FINDING SUCCESS IN LOVE AND WAFFLES

A Dash of Good

HOW TO TURN A BUSINESS BASED ON VALUES INTO A VALUABLE BUSINESS

Evan Dash

Copyright © 2024 Evan Dash.

All rights reserved. This book or parts thereof may not be reproduced in any form, stored in any retrieval system, or transmitted in any form by any means—electronic, mechanical, photocopy, recording, or otherwise—without prior written permission of the publisher, except as provided by United States of America copyright law. The use of quotations in a book review is permitted. For more information contact: books@storebound.com.

ISBN: 978-0-9971012-7-0 (Hardcover)

10 9 8 7 6 5 4 3 2 1

Library of Congress Cataloging-in Publication Data has been applied for.

This work depicts actual events in the life of the author as truthfully as recollection permits and/or can be verified by research. Occasionally, dialogue consistent with the character or nature of the person speaking has been supplemented. All persons within are actual individuals; there are no composite characters. The names of some individuals have been changed to respect their privacy.

All photos are by Evan Dash, with the exception of: insert page 2, top right, image courtesy of Lord & Taylor; insert page 2, middle & bottom left images licensed Shutterstock.com; insert page 8 lower left image courtesy of QVC, insert page 17 photos courtesy of Groupe SEB.

Cover illustration and book design by Amy Silverman-Miller.

Printed by StoreBound Books in China.

First hardcover edition July 2024.

StoreBound Books
50 Broad Street, 12th Floor
New York, NY 10004

bydash.com

Dedication

To my parents, Barbara & David Dash, for instilling the values of integrity, perseverance, and the pursuit of excellence. This book is a tribute to your love, guidance, and infinite patience.

And to Rachel, my co-founder, co-pilot, and soulmate. Your unwavering belief and boundless support along our journey have been my greatest strength. This story of growth, learning, and success would have been impossible without you.

Contents

FOREWORD 1
   by Geoffrey Zakarian

INTRODUCTION 5

1. **TRIAL BY FIRE** 13
2. **AUTHENTICITY MAKES AN IMPRESSION** 29
3. **EXCEED EXPECTATIONS** 47
4. **PEOPLE MAKE THE DIFFERENCE** 57
5. **EVERY DAY IS A JOB INTERVIEW** 67
6. **STORYTELLING AND SEAFOOD** 75
7. **RESPECT** 83
8. **WIN-WINS** 95
9. **BURNING DOWN THE HOUSE** 103
10. **CLARITY** 115
11. **PERFECTLY PAIRED** 123
12. **DON'T BE AN ENTREPRENEUR WITHOUT AN OFFERING** 129
13. **FROM VISION TO VENTURE** 145
14. **MONEY DOESN'T GROW ON TREES** 155

15. FROM RED-EYES TO REALIZATIONS	**163**
16. CHOOSE DISCIPLINE OVER DISARRAY	**171**
17. YOU ARE THE BRAND	**181**
18. WRITE A SURVIVAL STORY	**193**
19. IF YOU DON'T LEARN FROM FAILURE, YOU'RE JUST FAILING	**201**
20. PARTNERSHIPS & MULTIPLIERS	**209**
21. NO CULTURE, NO COMPANY	**219**
22. TRUST AND EMPOWERMENT UNLEASH POTENTIAL	**229**
23. GO THE EXTRA MILE	**239**
24. TURNING SOLID VALUES INTO HIGH MARKET VALUE	**251**
IN LOVING MEMORY OF MATTHEW DASH	**257**
WITH MY DEEPEST GRATITUDE	**259**

Foreword

by Geoffrey Zakarian

"The kitchen is a realm of endless possibilities where imagination and technique collide to create magic. As chefs, we are dreamers and craftsmen, sculpting our visions onto the canvas of taste. Each dish is a manifestation of our creativity, a testament to our journey, and an invitation for others to share in the experience."

—Geoffrey Zakarian, Iron Chef and Restaurateur

When I first entered the Culinary Institute of America, I didn't imagine a future as an author or TV personality. I didn't have my sights set on Michelin Stars or Emmy Nominations. I certainly wasn't chasing money or fame. My dream was quite simple—to become a great chef and connect with people through the magic of culinary experiences.

Upon graduation, I was set on learning from the world's finest chefs. So, I gathered my courage and knocked on the door of the famed Le Cirque in New York City and asked for a job, telling the executive chef I would work for free. I started my culinary journey the very next day and gave it everything I had.

While my peers were off to the beach during summer holidays, I embarked on culinary adventures in France. Paris, Nice, Lyon—these legendary cities became my classrooms as I staged at revered restaurants. From early mornings to late nights, I toiled alongside some of the most acclaimed chefs in the world, soaking in their expertise.

Four years later, I proudly assumed the role of Chef de Cuisine at Le Cirque under Chef Alain Sailhac before we moved to the legendary 21 Club in Manhattan. Two years later, as Executive Chef, I opened 44 at The Royalton Hotel with Ian Schrager, the legendary entrepreneur and hotelier credited for the "boutique hotel" concept. It became an instant hot spot.

In 1994, I embarked on my second project with Ian Schrager, The Blue Door, at the iconic Delano Hotel in Miami Beach. This establishment became the spark that ignited South Beach's resurgence, all through the art of connecting with people and crafting unforgettable experiences.

Over the next three decades, my unwavering focus remained on creating exceptional moments and forging genuine connections. As I built Zakarian Hospitality into a global brand, I observed the world changing around me.

Life today is less personal. Human experiences get diluted by digital interactions. Empathy and genuine understanding often take a back seat to efficiency and expediency. The art of conversation, the joy of serendipitous encounters, and the depth of human connections have become increasingly rare commodities.

As a chef, restaurateur, and TV personality, my success has always hinged on authentic human connections. I relish face-to-face interactions and meaningful conversations. My mission is clear—whether through dining experiences or the content I create, I strive to foster genuine connections.

I find my greatest fulfillment in enriching the lives of those I connect with.

In a global enterprise with millions of transactions all around the world, making business feel personal is a monumental undertaking. Evan Dash proves that with the right values and culture, you can do just that.

As I got to know Evan through his kitchen products company, it was refreshing to find a leader who understands that success goes beyond profits and products. It's about people—the heart and soul of any enterprise. I can't help but draw parallels between the art of cooking and the art of running a business. Both require precision, creativity, and a deep respect for the ingredients—whether spices in the kitchen or the individuals on your team.

Evan has demonstrated time and again that doing right by people is not only a noble pursuit but a path to extraordinary success. It's a philosophy that has resonated with me throughout my career as a chef. In the fast-paced world of restaurants and television, I've learned that the true recipe for success isn't just about the perfect dish; it's about a great team, the ideal partnerships, and the perfect blend of ingredients.

In this inspiring book, Evan shares his journey, insights, and secrets to building a thriving business that values people above all else. He doesn't merely talk the talk; he walks the walk. From nurturing talent within his company to forging meaningful relationships with customers and partners, Evan's approach proves the power of human connections.

As a chef, I've always believed that the finest dishes come to life when the ingredients harmonize, when the blend of flavors shines, and when the result brings joy to those who savor it. Evan's approach to business is no different. He understands that a successful enterprise is a carefully crafted blend of talents and efforts, each playing its part to create something extraordinary.

Within the pages of this book, you'll discover the power of empathy, the importance of integrity, and the undeniable impact of putting people first. Evan Dash's story proves you can achieve remarkable success without sacrificing your principles. In fact, it's often the businesses that prioritize their values that achieve the greatest heights.

So, whether you're a seasoned entrepreneur, a budding business owner, or someone simply seeking career inspiration, I invite you to savor the wisdom and insights that Evan Dash offers. His journey proves that in business, as in the kitchen, doing right by people is the secret ingredient that transforms ordinary enterprises into extraordinary ones.

Warmly,
Geoffrey Zakarian
Iron Chef and Restaurateur

Introduction

THE UNLIKELY ENTREPRENEUR

In 2017, I was waiting to take the stage at the NASDAQ for the Next Great Consumer Brands conference. I was ready to present the story of Dash, my fast-growing kitchen products brand, to a packed auditorium filled with a who's who of potential investors.

I had never been so excited or nervous to take the stage. I scanned the room and made eye contact with tennis legend Venus Williams, who had just presented her brand, Eleven. Next, my eyes moved to the second row where the President of my company, Glenn De Stefano, sat. He caught my eye and gave me a reassuring nod. Next to him, the architect of our brand voice, Cat Reinhard, beamed her smile right at me. Next to her, my co-founder and soulmate, Rachel, smiled and whispered sotto voce, "You got this, babe."

I took a deep breath and a moment to reflect and realized I was a lucky man indeed. Then, I stepped up and gave my speech. In the hours after the event, we were inundated with meeting requests from venture funds, private equity firms, family offices, and institutions. We were in the best possible position; by that, I mean we didn't *need* anyone's money. But we were in the market for the right partner who could offer capital *and* the expertise and resources to help us grow to the next level.

The right partner was not in the audience that night, and while I didn't realize it then, that was pure luck. Our search for the right investor would continue for several more years. In the interim, our business grew over $100 million, and our achievements stacked up. After the Next Great Consumer Brand recognition, we appeared on INC's list of the fastest-growing companies for the second, third, and fourth consecutive years.

Next, we landed in the top 100 of the Entrepreneur 360 list, then finally in Crain's magazine's top 50 fastest-growing businesses. I even appeared as an investor on CNBC's primetime show, *Make Me a Millionaire Inventor,* where inventors pitch ideas in a far more forgiving environment than the Shark Tank.

I should have been riding high, but the success continually ushered in new pressures. Our growing consumer products company had an insatiable appetite for inventory, which demanded cash flow on a level that caused mental, emotional, and even physical strain. So, to fuel the growth, Rachel and I gobbled up more and more debt, each time personally guaranteeing the loans until we had pledged all we owned as collateral to cover a mere fraction of the $40 million line of credit we had borrowed.

In 2020, we were presented with the most enticing investment opportunity thus far. It was exactly what we were looking for. They would bring us the resources of an $8 billion public company, including forty manufacturing plants, over two thousand patents, and a global distribution network in over one hundred and fifty countries.

I stood at the most significant crossroads of my professional life. On the one hand, I loved the autonomy brought by owning 100% of my business. On the other hand, continuing the growth trajectory would take a level of resources I couldn't access without selling company shares.

As I weighed the decision before me, I couldn't help but appreciate the improbable situation I found myself in. I was not the guy voted most likely to succeed in my graduating class, yet here I was, the most unlikely entrepreneur on the planet.

I went to eight colleges. Yes, eight. I did this, not because I was obsessed with education but because that's what you do when you make a career of flunking out of school but still want a job that requires a degree. After failing out of college for the last time, my father and I sat in his car in the parking lot of a strip mall near Boston. He asked me to run a few errands with him, but I assumed the outing was to hold me hostage for another lecture on the importance of a college education.

Instead of another lecture likely to yield the same result as the previous four, my dad just looked at me, and with incredible intensity, he threw me a curveball. "You are going to be so successful once you get into the business world, Evan," he said, his eyes piercing my soul. "Just get the damn piece of paper so you can begin the amazing life ahead of you."

It was the first talk about college with my dad that got through to me—probably because it wasn't about academics this time. It was evident to everyone that I had no interest in being a scholar. This time, it was a window into my future, and in the moment, the idea of achieving success was everything to me.

I soon found the road to success was challenging and humbling—filled with the excitement of advancements, often followed by setbacks that felt insurmountable. It was a real-life game of chutes and ladders. Through it all, I remained focused on learning what was necessary to take the next step forward. And I stacked these learnings at every stage to help me climb to the next level.

In less than ten years—an impossibly short time in the corporate world—I worked my way up to senior vice president of Macy's, where I ran the multi-billion-dollar home products business. My team was responsible for buying and marketing our products in over 700 stores nationwide. I felt on top of the business world and began to visualize my next step up the ladder to president.

Instead of staying true to the values that fueled my career growth, I got cocky. I did what was best for myself and my team, not the company or the customer. And certainly not my boss. The faster I advanced, the cockier I got. Eventually, I got fired, and my entire world came crashing down.

It felt as though the very ground beneath me shifted. My heart sank into my stomach, heavy with the weight of worry. The gravity of the situation was the heaviest weight I had ever felt. I had a house, a mortgage, two young boys, and more responsibility than ever. For the first time, I would go home, not as a provider but as the bearer of grim news.

In that moment, engulfed in a whirlwind of fear, uncertainty, and a crushing sense of loss, I realized the daunting task ahead. It wasn't something I could quickly brush off. I had to turn inward to figure out where I'd gone wrong.

It was the first time since my dad's college talk that I accepted the blame. I was finally ready to take responsibility for my actions and their consequences. I spent some of my darkest days doing the difficult soul-searching necessary to understand how I could have sabotaged my career so severely.

Ironically, I had my breakthrough moment on Black Friday, the kickoff to the holiday shopping season, just three weeks after I'd gotten fired from Macy's, the inventor of Black Friday. As I watched people fighting over cheap stuff in understaffed stores, the lunacy of what retail had become sunk in. Years after that conversation with my dad in the car, I finally unlocked the secret to my long-term success—**doing right by people is great for business.**

I decided then that I would continue to pursue business success, but this time, I looked to my roots as a firefighter, the job I landed when I failed out of college the first time. It was the only time I felt like my work mattered because I made a difference in other people's lives every day. I realized what should have been so clear to me from the outset—lasting success is a product of enriching lives by serving others.

As a firefighter, I built genuine relationships on a foundation of authenticity, kindness, and empathy—the same things I'd seen lacking in corporate leadership. In the fire department, my days revolved around the needs of others. In business, however, my focus was the company's goals, which had little bearing on the lives of others. My efforts were for someone else's vision of success—faceless shareholders I would never meet—and most days, I felt unfulfilled.

I promised that if I could get back on my feet, I would devote myself to finding satisfaction and success in helping others. The values I first embraced in the fire department 20 years earlier would become my bedrock, and my eventual success would be a product of my loyalty and advocacy for others.

Armed with a new awareness, Rachel and I became business founders in 2010. On the day we founded the company, I told her, "If we're lucky enough to get this off the ground, and on the off chance we actually have customers, we must do whatever it takes to make them fall in love with us."

Rachel wholeheartedly agreed, and from that moment forward, our mindset was one of genuine gratitude for everyone who would become part of our success story, no matter how big or small. Then, we turned that mindset of gratitude into an obsession with winning the hearts of everyone we encountered.

We would go the extra mile to win the hearts of our team by cultivating an inspired culture and empowering them to do great work. We would win the hearts of our retail customers by solving their problems and improving their results. And we would win the hearts of end consumers all around the globe by inspiring them and enriching their lives. These consumers would become our marketing department—advocating for us, spreading the love, and eventually purchasing our products well into the tens of millions of units and using them in their daily lives.

Our once lean and nimble startup has evolved into a complex enterprise, but our entrepreneurial spirit remains intact. Our obsession with maintaining the culture we cultivated is top of mind, and our relentless pursuit of winning hearts continues to guide our actions.

Our "overnight success" has been the culmination of over 40 years of life lessons, mostly learned the hard way. Like most people, I experienced giant setbacks that felt insurmountable, but looking back, I'm thankful for the knocks I've taken because each time, I got up more competent and more determined. Only after I committed myself to a winning hearts mindset did I begin to appreciate how the powerful lessons I learned throughout my life came together into the winning hearts strategy that enabled our success.

My objective in the chapters ahead is to outline a better way of doing business that anyone can apply to their career. I'll walk you through some of the most important lessons that shaped my approach to business. These lessons, combined with our overall secret sauce—a winning hearts mindset—were the key to turning our strong values-based business into a valuable enterprise.

Of course, there are the basics, like acting with integrity, leading by example, and empowering others. But there are many more nuanced lessons I learned throughout the years, from the playground to the boardroom, and there were so many influential mentors along the way—often in the unlikeliest of places who taught me what it means to find happiness and success even though I was the most unlikely entrepreneur in the world.

So let's get started.

1. Trial By Fire

I am a conventional man who wound up on an unconventional path. I wasn't born for the road less traveled—quite the contrary. I was always searching for stability and craving predictability—like a steady job and paycheck on direct deposit every two weeks. I'm a company man. That's why I chose to work for legacy companies—Fortune 500 retail giants who had withstood the test of time.

Corporate life laid opportunities before me. At just 30 years old, I had worked my way up the ladder to senior vice president of Macy's. And yet, I just couldn't settle in. I was too restless, too impulsive, too this or too that. I didn't fit the mold, although I desperately wanted to. It's been the same issue for me since Kindergarten. I was, as my mother would generously put it, a handful.

When open school night rolled around in first grade, my parents entered the classroom, searching for my seat. All the desks were arranged into tidy groups of four, and each one had an art project waiting cheerfully for the parents to admire. My parents made their way around the classroom two or three times, clearly lost.

"You must be Mr. and Mrs. Dash," my teacher finally said to my folks with a sympathetic smile. "Evan's desk is over here." She motioned them over to a desk on its own and adjacent to her desk in the front of the room. It had a floor-standing map shielding it from the view of the rest of the class. She had brilliantly created a mini classroom for me, sans distractions and without an audience.

If you have a child, you've heard stories about "that kid" in school. Well, that was me. Throughout elementary school, I spent much of my time isolated in the hall outside my classroom.

In middle school, my coping mechanism turned out to be athletics. Sports got me out of exile by providing an outlet for my energy and an incentive for good grades and behavior. I played football in the fall, basketball in the winter, and ice hockey in the spring. I thrived on physical activity, and being a part of something bigger than myself was exactly what I needed. I loved being part of a team, practicing with teammates, executing a strategy together, and competing to win. Sports brought a sense of harmony, order, reason, and connection into my life—all things I couldn't find in the classroom.

Each year brought me new lessons and greater responsibility. Stephen Shackel, my varsity basketball coach, made it clear that we represented our school and could not take the responsibility lightly. He taught me that appearances mattered. We wore suits and ties to school on game days and entered the gym looking like professionals who meant business. We made sacrifices for the team. We gladly offered our time, bodies, social lives, and sense of personal style in exchange for the pride of putting on the uniform and competing for our school.

My parents finally saw me do something at school that didn't involve causing trouble. I even brought home report cards that made them smile. I took responsibility for myself, controlled my behavior, and directed my energy into something positive, which put me on the right track.

By senior year, I was captain of the basketball team. When I graduated, I had offers to play college ball at Division III schools. Choosing one of those would have been the right choice, but being true to my competitive self, I decided to roll the dice and try to make the Division I team at UMass, where legendary coach John Calipari had just taken the helm. One of his first moves was to cut yours truly from the team. My college basketball career was over before it even began.

I wasn't good enough to play on that team, and I knew it the first time I stepped onto the court. It's useless to beat yourself up over something you can't change, so I transferred to Lehigh University, hoping to play the following year. In the interim though, without a team and competition, I lost the core of my identity. Lacking the structure I had come to rely on, I flunked out—not once, but twice. It felt like I was back in the hallway in grade school, sitting out my education in exile. Only now, I was a grown man searching for a new purpose in life.

I found it at a Fire Department in Bethlehem, Pennsylvania. I was always fascinated by fire trucks. My world would stop whenever I saw those shiny red engines with their sparkling silver accents racing past. Everything around me froze as I watched the firemen scream by on their way to rescue someone from something terrible. I thought it must be the most fantastic job in the world.

Landing a job at the local fire department excited me to accomplish something again. It was a physically demanding job, which I always enjoyed; it was all about teamwork, and the job even required a uniform. The pride came flooding back.

I remember the first time I pulled on my fireman's gear, standing in the equipment rack next to Engine 822. I was surprised at how heavy it was, 85 pounds —and that's before all the layers got soaked in sweat. DuPont engineered the coat and trousers. The outer shell blended NOMEX® for flame resistance and KEVLAR® for strength. The pants were worn chest-high to ensure enough overlap with the coat so your midsection wasn't exposed to the flames.

Heavy-duty red suspenders still hold up the trousers —a nod to the tradition of American firemen of the early 1800s. Tradition is everywhere in a firehouse, particularly in Bethlehem, the oldest professional fire brigade in the country. They imported their first engine from London in 1760, a rustic horse-drawn wagon called The Perseverance, which still sits on display in the nearby Moravian Museum.

Most of the crew in my station were second or third-generation firefighters and had grown up in a world where you run into a burning building—of course you do. You're a fireman, the son and grandson of firemen. It's in your blood.

I hadn't grown up in the brotherhood. My father worked in retail, a three-alarm fire of a different sort. To compensate for lost time, I immersed myself in training to develop the skills and expertise I needed to prepare for anything. The job was, first and foremost, to *solve the problem*—any problem.

Within a few months, I started gaining comfort on the job. I tried to fill those boots daily and serve with honor and tenacity. My teammates recognized this and helped me along—mostly by teasing me unmercifully every time I made a mistake. But then they showed me the right way because they needed to depend on me. Every firefighter needed those beside them to know as much and care as much as they did. A firehouse is a self-generating and self-reinforcing culture that favors competition—against fire, not each other. It oozes camaraderie.

As soon as you put on a fireman's helmet, you owe something to the generations of firefighters who have worn the helmet before you. The iconic helmet you see on today's firefighters was dubbed the "New Yorker" when it was first developed in 1830 by luggage maker and volunteer firefighter Henry Gratacap. Little has changed in the general shape. It still features a high peak front adorned with a company identifier and eight ribbed sections around the dome with an extended rear brim to channel water away from your neck. Almost 200 years of technological advancements have not altered Henry Gratacap's original design.

No matter where you go in America, big city or small town, the helmet is the same. It does more than protect the person wearing it. It's a powerful brand symbol that, for two centuries, has signaled that you are now in capable hands *no matter how grave the situation.*

The helmet was the first memorable lesson I learned about the power of a brand. If you failed in the task, you not only lost lives, you tarnished the brand. Wearing it was a great honor, and it came with great responsibility.

Despite the legacy traditions and camaraderie, life in the firehouse wasn't nonstop high-stakes emergencies and rescues. We didn't spend most days saving lives but rather in preparation—cleaning the trucks, checking the equipment, testing the hoses, and waiting for bells to ring that usually didn't. When the alarm did sound, it was most often a call to help someone who was having a bad day.

Our culture was one of genuine compassion for those we served. I learned that small gestures of kindness are as important as life-saving rescue operations. I gave hugs to new drivers hysterical about a fender bender. I bandaged children's scraped knees, then put them on the firetruck to make their day. I held the hands of elderly patients en route to the hospital with injuries from a fall. I even climbed into an attic to help a squirrel family return to the outside world, giving the grateful homeowners a good night's sleep for the first time in weeks. No matter the trivial or tragic task, when I wore the helmet, I embodied the brand. I carried the legacy.

Beyond the technical skills, being a firefighter taught me to live up to the reputation of a legacy brand. It taught me that you can only be part of the solution, never part of the problem. And you never walk away from a task until you reach the best possible outcome. Failure is never an option.

As I gained experience, I grew ravenous to devour all the knowledge I could. At night, I continued business studies at local colleges. I read book after book on fire science and emergency services management daily. I completed every training class offered. I got certified as a firefighter, emergency medical technician, and vehicle rescue specialist. I earned certificates in high-angle cliff and water rescue.

While real emergencies were few and far between, there were critical moments when lives were on the line. In the moment, all the training, preparation, and team building came together.

One such moment occurred on a beautiful September afternoon. I was about a year into the job. It was one of those days when I liked being a junior guy assigned to clean the trucks outside the big bay garage doors. A breeze with the first crisp hint of fall was biting back the heat of summer. Suddenly, the station radio squawked to life.

In a firehouse, the radio is always droning on in the background. No one pays much attention until you hear a unique sequence of tones signaling an emergency dispatch. Each fire department has unique tones that precede essential information. The brain quickly recognizes these tones over the chatter, and firefighters react as though someone is shouting their name.

"Dispatch to station 8-2-0. Multiple callers reporting motor vehicle accident on I-78. Possible entrapment."

Our station sprang into action. Hearing "multiple callers," I raced to the equipment rack and was fully dressed before dispatch finished the call. It was serious business if the dispatch center received multiple simultaneous calls about an incident.

"Roll 826!" Assistant Chief Barndt shouted, telling us what we already knew—our heavy rescue unit would be first out of the station. We had performed this routine together countless times. We knew the checklist by heart, yet we went through the formalities step by step to ensure we missed nothing in those first critical moments.

Heavy Rescue 826 screamed out of the driveway, lights on, sirens blaring. A million-dollar, state-of-the-art mobile rescue unit and command center, 826 was our new 7-person marvel of modern technology. Powered by a Detroit Diesel 515hp motor, the unit was equipped with 30-kilowatt generators and a light tower with weather monitoring that could extend 30 feet above the truck and light up the darkest scene as brightly as a summer day. The back of the cab became our incident control command center, with a desktop computer and mobile fax machine. It was as much a marvel to us in the 1990s as Perseverance had been to the inhabitants of Bethlehem in 1760.

On board, we carried a full complement of hydraulic rescue tools: the Jaws of Life, low- and high-pressure airbags capable of lifting a semi-truck, and rescue struts to stabilize several tons of twisted metal while we attended to the victims. The truck also carried the necessities for more specialized situations, like high-angle rope gear, water rescue equipment, and a high-pressure cascade system to refill our Scott air packs for breathing, which were mounted right into each of our seats. The driver even had a truck-mounted breathing system to provide fresh air when the scene was contaminated.

We covered a long stretch of I-78, including busy interchanges prone to mishaps, so we didn't take our modern technology for granted. And that day, we needed every bit of technology at our disposal.

En route to the scene, we were part of a web of rapid communication and planning. Our unit communicated with the dispatch center. We coordinated with other apparatus from our department and exchanged information with our cross-functional teams, like the police and EMS. Our well-rehearsed choreography came to life as we raced to the accident scene. We mainly spoke in verbs. There was no time for modifiers or adjectives. We used language with the brevity and succinctness absent in the business world.

"Dash, Deegan, prep the Jaws," said Captain Martin. "Doddy, Babigian, on medical with me—grab the O2. I got the crash kit." The communication was crystal clear in our headsets, isolated from the truck's engine and siren's wail.

My team of four rode shoulder to shoulder, facing backward in the large rear cab of the truck. We knew the men up front would position the apparatus and stop traffic, ensuring safety in the first critical minutes. They would neutralize hazards and stabilize the vehicles while we attended to the victims.

"826 to PD, advise update," Martin spoke into his mic.

Clear communication with responding police was essential. Our strong relationship with the local PD allowed both departments to execute with precision.

"PD 175 to 826," the radio squawked back. "Highway access gate open. Two units in place. Traffic stopped. Four additional units and State PD en route to scene. Three-minute ETA."

Within minutes of the initial dispatch, all responding personnel assignments were clear. I felt the adrenaline pumping through my veins as I reviewed the checklist for prepping the Jaws of Life.

"Quarter mile to scene, no sign of smoke," Captain Martin said, breaking the silence. "Traffic stopped, clear path along median. Exit left side."

As soon as we arrived, I jumped off the truck and made a quick assessment to avoid tunnel vision. The pickup truck was a gnarl of twisted metal. While Doddy and Babigian made an initial assessment of the victim, I headed for our equipment bay and the hydraulic tools.

"Medical command to base, fly the bird," Doddy spoke into his radio.

"Roger medical command, Medevac dispatched," the radio squawked back. The helicopter was on its way. "ETA seven minutes."

As additional units arrived, police shut the highway and placed large orange cones to designate the helicopter's landing zone.

Deegan fired up the hydraulic pump while I laid out our cutting tools, and Doddy and Martin worked to stabilize the patient. Arriving personnel focused on their own tasks. Our Chief arrived on the scene and took charge.

"Incident Command to Medic-76. One male patient. Roughly 40. In and out of consciousness. Thready pulse," Chief Csaszar relayed over the radio to the paramedics about to arrive on the scene.

Collectively, Fire Chief Bill Csaszar and Assistant Chief Thomas Barndt had a calming and confidence-boosting effect, even in the most intense emergencies. When the Chief rolled in, he'd make an assessment and relay it over the radio with the soothing composure of a late-night DJ. The Chief's demeanor always brought down tensions, ensuring clear thinking, even in the worst situations. Barndt, on the other hand, was more drill sergeant— the perfect counter-balance to the Chief. Tommy's orders were clear and unwavering, leaving nothing to chance. His knack for rapidly gauging situations and directing the right actions was unmatched. Serving under these two leaders instilled a sense of clarity, confidence, and an aspiration to lead like them someday.

The first EMS crew brought equipment, including an orange backboard that we would use to shield the driver from breaking glass or metal debris as we cut the vehicle away from him.

Deegan and I positioned the Jaws and popped off the passenger door like we were opening a sardine can. Doddy moved into the vehicle, kneeling on the inside of the roof of the upside-down truck. The dashboard pinned the driver's legs. He was hanging upside down.

The situation was precarious. Once we relieved the vehicle's pressure, our patient could succumb to internal bleeding previously controlled by the force of being pinned. We kept cutting away twisted metal until Martin pointed to where we would use the hydraulic spreader to bend the dashboard off our patient.

With a neck immobilizer secured, Doddy made room for a paramedic to start an IV in our patient's arm. The paramedic backed out and gave the group of 10 or 12 firefighters clear instructions to support the patient and bring him down gently as we freed his legs and completed the extrication.

With the helicopter circling the landing zone, Deegan and I positioned the spreader between the vehicle frame and the underside of the dashboard. As we slowly pried the dashboard off the driver's legs, four additional firemen supported him until we could gently guide him onto the backboard.

We positioned our patient, secured him to the board, and carried him away from the wreck. Simultaneously, the Medevac helicopter landed, and its crew hustled toward us with their stretcher.

We placed the board with our patient onto the stretcher, then carefully secured MAST pants onto his legs. These MAST pants, short for Military Anti-Shock Trousers, could be inflated in-flight to push the patient's blood volume from the lower extremities and pelvis to the critical organs in the upper body, potentially extending survival until a blood transfusion at the trauma center.

Doddy and I wheeled the stretcher to the helicopter for a "hot load." With the rotors still spinning, we approached the chopper from the front to avoid the deadly tail rotor. The back bay doors opened, and we loaded the stretcher until the fasteners snapped into place. The crew boarded, and as the doors closed, the turbines grew deafening. We all took a knee on the highway with our backs to the chopper so the downwash from the rotors wouldn't blow us over. As the wind subsided, I looked up and saw the helicopter maneuver into a nose-dipped position to maximize its horizontal thrust. It quickly gained speed as it flew toward the helipad on the roof of the Lehigh Valley Hospital Trauma Center.

As the chopper faded into the distance, I began to settle down inside. It was time to stow gear, reopen the highway, and return to the station to debrief. As I stared at the wrecked truck, a knot of twisted metal, Doddy slapped me on the back and exclaimed, "He squeezed my hand, Dash."

I turned around and Doddy gave me a giant smile. Flush with the excitement and adrenaline of having just saved a life, he shouted again, "He squeezed my hand!"

We had an incredible outcome that day. On other days, the results were not so terrific.

After six years on the job, I made Assistant Captain, but a different kind of fire still burned inside me: an ambition to trade my hook and ladder for the corporate ladder. My experiences in the fire service honed my character and set the stage for the business aspirations that pulled at me.

I finally earned enough credits from those eight different colleges to graduate from one—Moravian College. With a degree under my belt, I applied for the executive training programs of large corporations in New York City.

A change of this magnitude wasn't an easy decision. To leave behind a life carved with dedication, memories, and irreplaceable camaraderie felt almost sacrilegious. But I was poised to dive into the business world, and while the challenges ahead were different, they would feel strangely familiar. After all, everything I needed to know about business was already learned on the back of a firetruck.

Takeaways
TRIAL BY FIRE

- **Turn setbacks into comebacks.**
  Mark Twain said, "Find a job you enjoy doing, and you'll never work a day in your life." I transformed from an academic trainwreck to a successful professional by doing work that mattered to me. Belonging to a team didn't just offer me a role; it presented purpose, responsibility, and a platform to shine. The fire department channeled my scattered energies toward something that mattered. It unlocked my potential to make significant contributions and to excel on my chosen path, which was about to change from emergency services to business.

- **Teamwork breeds success.**
  Leadership roles provided me with an appreciation for the remarkable achievements that teams can attain, surpassing the potential of any one individual. I became a student of team dynamics and obsessed over the common characteristics of great teams: alignment of goals, rigorous planning and practice, clear communication, and strong, selfless leadership. It's no coincidence that great teams invariably produce remarkable outcomes.

- **Confident leadership has a ripple effect.**
  Authentic confidence, free of bravado, is built upon capability and self-awareness. When leaders are grounded in their abilities and confident in

their judgments, they foster a cascading trust that trickles down to all levels. Strong leaders who communicate with confidence create a wave of collective confidence throughout their team. They do more than simply lead; they ignite a chain reaction of belief, ambition, and achievement. They also serve as a role model for aspiring leaders, providing a blueprint for success that others can emulate.

- **A brand must be respected and protected.**
  A great brand is memorable, meaningful, and forges an emotional connection. Developing a robust brand identity requires a profound dedication to serving the needs of those it seeks to satisfy. The fire department brand radiated competence and inspired trust, anchored in traditions and values that had endured for almost three centuries. This cultural ethos permeated every action, leaving no doubt as to our obligation to safeguard the equity of our brand.

- **Precision over haste.**
  To a casual onlooker, a firetruck racing to a scene paints a picture of urgency and chaos. In reality, it epitomizes a meticulous plan in motion, precisely choreographed and designed to save lives. The combination of robust planning and routine practice is the only route to great results. Our preparation for every imaginable emergency ensured if the day ever came, performing with precision would be second nature.

- **Celebrate, then evolve.**
  Every victory, whether in sports or a life-saving mission, deserves its moment of glory. Those small moments of gratitude reinforced our hard work and boosted camaraderie and morale. However, we never allowed success to become a gateway to complacency. After every endeavor, we debriefed, free of finger-pointing, and with our emotions checked at the door. We had each other's backs, and everyone knew it. This allowed each teammate to welcome constructive feedback, fostering an environment of perpetual growth.

2. Authenticity Makes an Impression

The pursuit was on. A challenging and rewarding business career in New York City had always been my dream. Lord & Taylor's executive training program held a reputation as the nation's finest. I was heading into Manhattan for an interview with the iconic retailer, seeking one of 20 coveted spots.

I took the train from Allentown to Penn Station. As I approached number 424 on Fifth Avenue, my feelings were hard to describe precisely. Let's settle for *awestruck*.

Lord & Taylor spanned a city block, from 38th to 39th Streets—11 stories of gleaming white limestone, masterfully framed by Italian Renaissance columns. Golden window sashes gleamed in crisp rays of Manhattan sunlight. The magnificent main doors opened onto Fifth Avenue.

I had arrived an hour early, eager to size up the place that billed itself as America's first and greatest department store. As the clock on the building struck noon, it seemed that every door up and down Fifth Avenue opened at once, spilling streams of workers into one massive mad dash for lunch.

The competitive current of Manhattan life almost lifted me off my feet as the heart of the shopping district filled with people and sounds: the squeal of brakes, blaring cab horns, yelps of hotdog and pretzel barkers, all underscored by the subterranean rumble of the subway. It was beautiful music to me, the city's symphony beating out its staccato rhythm, repeating the chorus over and over—time is money. Time is money. New York City is hardwired to teach that lesson, and I found it exhilarating.

As I passed the main display windows, with their mannequins decked out in classic Lord & Taylor style—another way of saying *classic American style*—it felt like I was coming home, only to a place I had never been. It felt like a dream, pushing through the massive revolving doors beneath four mammoth American flags fluttering over Fifth Avenue like an omen of good things to come.

I knew the flags were there thanks to the iconic Dorothy Shaver, Lord & Taylor's CEO through its golden era, the first woman in the country to run a multi-million-dollar corporation. Shaver held the reins at Lord & Taylor from 1927 until she died in 1959. She was a skilled merchant with an intuition for the fashion that New York women would find irresistible. Under Shaver, Lord & Taylor was the first department store to feature separate departments for teens, young adults, petite women, career women, and brides. She created the first maternity department because she was determined to dress women to feel wonderful through every stage of their lives.

She upgraded the shopping experience by introducing personal shoppers and the novel idea of opening restaurants right inside the store, so ladies who lunched never had to leave the store. Then, she created the first suburban department store in Stamford, Connecticut, and ensured it had the same classic elegance as the Manhattan flagship.

Shaver grew Lord & Taylor from $2 million in revenue to $100 million the year she died. She enshrined Lord

& Taylor as *THE* destination for American women with style. Shaver helped establish New York City as a fashion capital by featuring American designers and shaping Lord & Taylor's signature "American Look."

As I entered the store, the aroma of pricey cosmetics and age-defying lotions filled my senses. I stood on the marble floor for a moment, soaking up the elegance, the flair, the New York style. I must have looked like a tourist, gawking up at the ornate ceiling, blocking the flow of foot traffic.

"Ladies, Lancôme has a gift for you today with any $75 purchase," said a flawlessly dressed sales associate.

"Good afternoon, sir," another elegant young woman greeted me. She was holding a blue glass bottle shaped like a male torso. "Have you tried the new Gaultier Le Male? Free aftershave with any purchase."

I fled the fragrant cloud and made my way to the escalators. As I rode up to Human Resources on nine, I took a bird's eye view of each floor. The store's scale was overwhelming, but the organization of the departments made it manageable. You could find exactly what you were looking for here and, of course, discover much more along the way.

Each escalator brought me to a marble landing with a styled vignette suggesting what one could find on that floor. Arriving on nine, I was greeted by three bespoke mannequins wearing the crispest shirts I had ever seen. As I passed the judgmental polystyrene, I thought I saw one of the dummies roll his eyes at my Today's Man factory outlet suit.

I circled the floor several times before making my way to the HR offices. The butterflies in my stomach turned into velociraptors as I opened the HR door and approached an elegant receptionist.

"I'm Evan Dash. I'm here for an interview."

"Welcome, Mr. Dash."

The receptionist was the prologue to the high-end retailer's story. She wore a tailored, dove-gray dress that flattered her silhouette. The neckline had subtle yet intricate beadwork, which shimmered in the light each time she moved. A refined gold watch and delicate earrings added a touch of elegance.

Her ensemble was her version of the firefighter's helmet, embodying the essence of the upscale brand she worked for. She was more than a receptionist—she personified the retailer's identity, nailing her fashion moment and leaving an indelible mark on everyone who walked into that office.

"Our vice president is expecting you. I'll let him know you're here." She offered a reassuring smile and motioned to the seating area. As she disappeared, I sat and reflected on what I'd seen on my way up to nine. I'd done my due diligence to prepare for the interview, but being there brought it all to life. Lord & Taylor's mission was to fulfill their customers' aspirations to present the best version of themselves. They had been doing that for generations, and I wanted to be a part of it. It felt challenging, worthwhile, and almost magical.

A door in the paneling opened, and Jim Viola, Vice President of Human Resources, came toward me, hand outstretched. He wore a grey pinstriped suit, crisp white shirt, and sapphire blue tie. His shoes were polished to a military shine. And he was younger than I'd expected, with friendly blue eyes.

It was inspiring to encounter someone in his early thirties who had already achieved success at a senior level.

"Let's go back to my office and talk," Jim said.

I followed him to his office, where two visitor chairs faced his desk with his executive chair behind it. Jim hung his suit jacket on the back of his door. I kept mine on and sat down, trying to look cool, calm, and collected —the opposite of what I felt.

"I came early to spend time in the store," I told him. "It's awe-inspiring."

I'd figured it was wise to underline my punctuality, but Jim Viola seemed unmoved. Leaning back in his chair, he folded his arms. His body language seemed to be saying, *Okay kid, cut the crap, let's hear it.*

I froze, and for what felt like a terrifying eternity, neither of us said a word. There was only the hum of Manhattan floating up from Fifth Avenue.

Finally, Mr. Viola spoke. "So, Evan. Why the interest in Lord & Taylor?"

He came across like a busy executive trying not to sound impatient.

"I went to school for business. I want a career in retail, and I want to work for the best."

I wanted to claw back those banalities as soon as I'd uttered them. I'd laid it on too thick, and Jim Viola had heard it all before.

Instead, I kept on talking, too much, too fast. What Lord & Taylor and American style signified to me. How much I respected the tradition of innovation, yada, yada. I couldn't stop blabbering. And, of course, it only made things worse. Jim Viola wasn't saying a word, just watching me flailing in deep water, too polite to tell me to shut up. I was way over my head and getting deeper.

I was running out of superlatives in my gushing and unnecessary review of Lord & Taylor's history. "I interviewed at A&S last week!" I babbled. "Mr. Belz at A&S told me the Executive Training Program at Lord & Taylor is the best in the country, so this is where I want to learn."

At my interview with Abraham & Strauss, another iconic department store, Brad Belz, their head of HR, had asked where else I was interviewing. When I mentioned Lord & Taylor, he smiled and told me that he had developed the executive training program at L&T himself and that it was second to none.

Jim sat forward with a smile. "I know Brad well! I used to work for him here. He built our training program."

I had managed to find one little thread connecting Mr. Viola and me. It was like finding a buoy to cling to in a rugged sea. But it wasn't enough. For the next 20 minutes, Jim peppered me with questions, and I provided all-too-predictable answers.

Somehow, I had to separate myself from the pack; otherwise, I would get that form letter in a few days, thanking me for my time and regretfully informing me that I hadn't made the cut.

"Retail isn't for everybody," Jim remarked, already setting me up for an easy letdown. "It's a fast-paced, highpressure environment. So let me ask you, Evan, how do you handle stress?"

And that is when I saw my chance.

"I doubt we view stress the same way, Mr. Viola."

Maybe it sounded cocky, but I could tell I suddenly had his full attention.

"I mean, sir, are you talking about the stress people get from a to-do list that keeps growing? From an overflowing inbox? Competing priorities in a dynamic environment? Or are you talking about the type of stress I experienced as Assistant Captain of my fire department?"

He leaned even further forward. He was curious about what I had said.

"Well, I know there's office stress. But then there's the stress you feel at three o'clock in the morning, jumping off a fire engine in front of a burning house with kids on the second floor and people screaming. Or pulling up to an accident scene on the interstate with a gnarl of twisted metal that was once a vehicle, gasoline all over the road, and victims clinging to life. So, how do I handle stress? I thrive on it. It's my fuel. It brings out the best in me."

He had locked in. "Tell me more."

"I've experienced the intensity of life and death situations where I had to make decisions in an instant. As a first responder, you have to grasp the entire picture quickly. An emergency scene is always dynamic, never static. You need to absorb a lot of information fast, make an assessment, and develop a game plan. You have mere seconds to consider all the factors. Are there people in the building? Are downed wires touching the wrecked car? Can the victim survive transport by ground, or do we need to fly them? The list is long. And if you succumb to tunnel vision or let incoming information overwhelm you, or you just crumble under the stress, people can die."

Jim was taking in what I had said. I could tell it meant something to him.

"But it can't be like that all the time?" he asked. "What about the follow-up after an emergency? What about budgeting, team dynamics, maintenance, and preparation? How do you handle the more mundane parts of the job?"

"A huge amount of administration and management comes with the job. Somebody's always breathing down your neck, and often, before you finish the reports, you get another call. I don't sweat that kind of pressure. When you have just extricated a 5-year-old from a crushed Mazda, handling the other responsibilities of the job seems a lot easier. It's all about perspective."

"That's amazing!" Jim said with excitement in his voice.

The form letter dismissing me from contention might have just hit the circular file. And sure enough, the next day, Jim Viola called personally to offer me a spot on the Lord & Taylor executive training program. A few days later, my welcome package arrived, including my first perk —an employee discount card. To celebrate, I returned to Lord & Taylor and bought some new work clothes.

Six weeks later, I arrived at the conference room on the eighth floor of the store. It was the first day of the program, and a group of executive trainees already waited to check in. Everyone was young, outgoing, and very much pulled together. Jim Viola had hand-picked us. We had each made an impression that landed us a spot in that room.

When the doors opened, we took seats around a giant U-shaped table and waited silently until a tall brunette rushed into the room.

"Good morning everyone. I'm LJ Gallagher." She was out of breath. "Sorry if I'm sounding a bit frazzled. Today's my first day back from maternity leave. I'll be leading this program for the next 12 weeks."

The pace was quick. Things unfolded rapidly. I was no longer that troublesome grade school kid. I preferred to think of myself as lively, so the environment already seemed like a good fit.

LJ spent the next hour outlining the training program. Our curriculum would combine classroom lessons, on-the-job training in the buying office, and working on the sales floor. Sessions in the classroom would flow into real-life situations as we worked alongside our buyers to create the seamless Lord & Taylor customer experience.

This was the mid-1990s and no longer the heyday of the department store. I never experienced "the good ole days" when department stores ruled the retail roost. Specialty stores and big box retailers were on the rise, and off-price and discount retailers were making it impossible to compete on price. E-commerce was emerging and would set a new bar for customer convenience. Even supermarkets were selling department store-type merchandise.

The department store was already an endangered species—but you wouldn't have known it inside the L&T training program. All the panache that had put Lord & Taylor at the top of the retail world still shimmered from chandeliers lighting up the marble floors of a magnificent emporium where time seemed to stand still.

Though, of course, it didn't. It never does.

In our second week, the whole class was abuzz. We were receiving our buying department assignments. These would shape our experience in the coming months and perhaps even guide career tracks far into the future. The atmosphere felt like the first day of school. We were all eager to get started on our professional journeys.

About 50 additional people were in the room that day—buyers, associate buyers, and assistant buyers, all waiting to collect their new trainees. The assignments, as far as I knew, were random.

"Brian, Gifts. Scott, Men's Sportswear. Julie, Kids." As LJ called out the names and departments, one by one, my friends peeled off and joined their new mentors. "Jim, Women's Shoes. Jackie, Dresses." Until I was the last one left sitting at the table.

"Last but not least," said LJ, smiling at me—a little sardonically, I thought. I'd been hoping for Men's Dress Shirts or even Men's shoes or ties, but those slots had been filled. What was left?

"Evan Dash, Women's Sportswear."

Wait, WHAT? There must be some mistake. I didn't even know what women's sportswear was.

My new buyer and her assistant stepped forward to collect me. They seemed about as interested in me as I was in Women's Sportswear. On the bright side, they were both named Carol, so I had only one name to remember.

As we walked to their office, they were all business.

"You're lucky to be in this area. It's the focal point of the company," Carol #1, the buyer, said.

I smiled but suspected that this was what every buyer told their trainee.

Carol #2, the assistant, spoke up. "This is how it works. On Mondays, you will complete the selling reports. On Tuesdays, you enter price changes. On Wednesdays, you're back in the classroom."

The Carols looked at each other and rolled their eyes about "the classroom." It was like the cafeteria scene straight out of Mean Girls.

"On Thursdays, we do market appointments," assistant Carol continued. "While we're at the showrooms, you answer our phones."

Carol #2 then handed me a pile of printouts. I held them awkwardly, without realizing their significance, but buried in that cumbersome pile of paper was my future.

"Do I ever go to market appoin--"

"No." Carol #1 cut me off. "You don't come to the designer showrooms, Marc-"

"Uh, it's Evan."

"Whatever. You cover the phones and complete your assignments."

Like the alpha she was, Carol #1 made eye contact and held it, making sure I understood my place in the food chain. I nodded, which seemed to satisfy her, and she finished detailing the schedule.

"On Fridays, we wrap up and prepare for the next week, which is always busier than the one before."

"Our department is in full swing by 7:30 a.m.," assistant Carol said. "Never, ever be late. Ever. Most of us leave by 7:00 p.m., but you'll probably stay later. Count on it. You'll need more time since you don't know anything yet."

"Everything clear so far?" said Alpha Carol.

"Yes, definitely. And I'm looking forward to being a strong member of your team," I said, determined to sound confident. Basketball taught me never to show weakness when faced with intimidation. When bigger players tried to push me around, I let my actions respond, using agility, intelligence, and precise shooting to prove that underestimating me was a mistake.

But the Carols just exchanged glances and burst into sinister laughter. They knew I wouldn't be a strong member of their team. I'd be long gone before that would ever happen.

The first thing I learned about women's sportswear is that it had nothing to do with sports. Far from the trendy athleisure of today, women's sportswear, a term introduced to the fashion world by American designers, referred to clothing women wore to watch sports, not play them. Over time, these outfits evolved into something called Coordinated Separates, which, by the nineties, meant work attire for the professional woman.

My division was about 50 women, with a few men sprinkled in. The women arrived each day impeccably dressed in fashionable attire for the busy professional. Their accessories were pricey, with designer logos proclaiming the holy trinity of the G's: Gucci, Gaultier, and Givenchy. Men wore tailored suits, crisp shirts, and meticulously shined shoes.

My colleagues came from diverse backgrounds but had at least one thing in common—no one ever smiled. I smiled a lot, so fitting into that culture took effort.

As we approached the office on five, the Carols navigated the selling floor like two mice who knew precisely where to find their cheese, and I did my best to keep up. We took a final turn around the gleaming glamour of the sales floor before I followed them through nondescript doors into the sunless world of my new home. I could feel reality shifting under my feet as the plush carpet of the selling floor turned into thin, grungy industrial workplace carpeting. The grey walls looked cold under fluorescent light, tagged with years of scuff marks from carelessly wheeled clothing racks. It felt like going back to Kansas after a week in Oz. It was a shock. The scruffy environment screamed *tyranny and surrender!*

The floor plan was an open bullpen with workstations arranged around the perimeter where associate and assistant buyers sat. A gray Formica counter that might have been from a 1950s suburban kitchen held printers and a fax machine and offered a cramped workspace for assistant buyers. Wooden shelves sagged under the weight of countless black vinyl binders stuffed with various reports.

It was a low-tech workspace. There were three doors, each leading into a different buyer's office. Buyers were the big shots, the seasoned retail veterans who made all the decisions for their departments. They were the people who decided which shade of blue, saffron, or chartreuse the women on Fifth Avenue would wear to work each season.

That dingy, crowded office spoke of a culture that was cold and transactional. I didn't meet with Alpha Carol again for an entire week, even though I sat at the counter right outside her office. Even then, it was hardly a meeting—more like an encounter at a bus stop. Brief, hurried, almost meaningless.

As weeks passed, I became proficient at my menial tasks and started learning the business. Most days involved wrestling with the figures in those dispiriting plastic binders, but occasionally, I was allowed to accompany my boss to a meeting. Those days were exciting, but I could never predict when she would include me in her plans. Instead of giving me time to prepare, she would emerge from her office and simply nod in my direction, my cue to leap into action and follow her out the door.

I became adept at juggling binders, notepads, a calculator, and pencils while shrugging into my suit jacket and running after my boss as she sped across the sales floor like a woman on roller skates, firing questions at me over her shoulder.

"Did you finish the selling report? Key the price changes? Call Claiborne back? Fax the orders to Gianni?"

No matter how many times I answered "Yes," there was never a "good job, Evan." When you did your job, your reward was silence. We would only make eye contact at the moment before entering the meeting. Stopping short, she would turn and glare at me.

"Don't open your mouth unless I ask you something."

Then, she would turn on her heel and make her grand entrance.

The culture was a letdown. I was accustomed to a strong sense of camaraderie among my co-workers in the fire department. We relied on that connection; it made us all better at our jobs. We were a team, a work family—but this, this was not camaraderie; this was sibling strife with a vicious edge. It was *The Devil Wears Prada* on steroids years before the movie.

Twelve weeks into the training program, there was one final order of business before the executive training program concluded: the Chairman's Lunch. Our class was getting 45 minutes of the big man's time. We could each ask him a question.

"There are no stupid questions," LJ reassured us, but we all knew she meant precisely the opposite.

I'd always been a bit star-struck about CEOs. The leader of a massive organization was a daunting figure, a person of vision and courage. CEOs were authoritarian, no-nonsense leaders, omniscient and capable—like my parents when I was a kid. CEOs saw things more clearly and understood their business at a deeper level than the rest of us—they had to.

LJ had built up the Chairman's Lunch as the major event of the training program. On our last day, we spent the morning reflecting on our progress through the 12 weeks of training. Precisely at noon, the door to the conference room swung open, and an attractive young woman, impeccably dressed, entered, then held the door as the CEO strode into our midst.

He looked like he had stepped off the cover of Fortune Magazine and into our classroom. His gray trousers were perfectly pressed. He wore a blue Oxford cloth shirt with a white collar and white cuffs, the height of executive fashion at the time. Gold cufflinks sparkled in the light, which matched the gleam of the clips on his deep red paisley suspenders. His ensemble was pure Lord & Taylor, and he indeed looked the part.

To top it off, he was smoking a pipe.

"Damn," I remember thinking. "The rules don't apply to this guy!"

He took a seat at the center of the U-shaped seating arrangement. No one said a word. He sat for a moment, taking us all in. He wasn't smiling, but he wasn't frowning either. His gaze was like that of a capricious king who could take his time and ponder his possibilities. It was the gaze of someone who certainly had all the answers, even before he had heard the questions.

"Thank you so much for sharing your time with us," LJ said. She wasn't groveling, but almost. She then made a complete introduction, reminding us of our noble leader's many accomplishments.

He looked almost peeved, which surprised me. I probably would have been beaming if someone sang my praises like that.

When LJ finished, our CEO took the floor and pontificated on our good fortune to work for one of the most iconic companies in the world. His deep, booming voice echoed off the walls like God talking to Moses from the mountaintop.

In those days, Lord & Taylor was still woven into the fabric of American culture. The store's "Signature of American Style" catchphrase didn't happen by accident—L&T had earned that title, and we were told it was our responsibility to continue earning it every day. Lord & Taylor was the crown jewel in our owner's, the May Company's, portfolio of department stores, and it was on us to keep it that way.

Weeks before, we had submitted our questions to LJ for vetting. We were far too green and unpredictable to pose a question without initial filtering by somebody higher up the chain.

As our CEO concluded his speech, the atmosphere grew tense. Everyone was nervous about questioning the king.

LJ called on each trainee by name to ask their pre-approved questions.

Most were softballs.

Authenticity Makes an Impression | 43

"Why do you think Lord & Taylor is the best retailer?" Snore.

"What has allowed us to endure for over 100 years?" Already explained that.

"How many stores do you think is the right number for us to have?" A little more interesting, but still.

Naturally, he handled each of the questions smoothly, as you would expect the CEO to answer, as though he was graciously giving an interview to a junior reporter from the Wall Street Journal.

"Our final question is from Evan Dash," LJ announced, then looked straight at me like she was willing me not to go rogue.

By then, I had a reputation for saying what I thought. I wasn't rude, maybe just a bit more direct than my peers.

I stood up as each of my classmates had done. I was hungry to hear something real from him. I wanted something authentic about what it meant to be a leader.

"Sir, I noticed that we ran our first-ever 10 percent off coupon last month, and the sales results exceeded everyone's expectations."

He smiled and nodded his head.

"I also heard that we plan to run another coupon next month, and the expectation is even higher."

"That's right, young man. We are doing very well with the coupon strategy. Do you have a question?"

My approved question was whether he was pleased with the coupon strategy. But he'd already answered that, so I adjusted on the fly.

"Do you worry that we will train our customers to only shop with a coupon?"

Dead silence. Our CEO stared at me intensely as though he were trying to turn me into a pillar of salt. He lit his pipe and puffed a few times. His silence was almost tactile, like a weapon.

I began to get nervous, waiting to hear what he might say. All bets were off.

"Business is competitive, young man," he finally admitted. "We must try new things. Fear of training the customer to only shop with a coupon doesn't keep me awake at night. If it happens, it won't be my problem; it'll be the next guy's. In the meantime, our numbers go up, and our shareholders are happy."

I was shocked by the honesty of his answer. He admitted openly that the pressure for immediate results outweighed the long-term consequences. He acknowledged that his tenure at the helm was a passing thing, and then he would fade into history. Unfortunately, a few decades later, so would Lord & Taylor.

I respected the man for his candor. It offered real insight into the underlying conflict between short and long-term thinking in many legacy businesses. Two decades after that Chairman's Lunch, Lord & Taylor was owned by the Hudson Bay Trading Company and struggling to survive. In 2019, with limited options, the company sold the iconic Flagship at 424 Fifth Avenue to WeWork, founded in 2010 by two guys in Brooklyn, which at that moment was, briefly, worth billions. Less than a year later, WeWork crashed and sold 424 Fifth Avenue to Amazon—another illustration of how quickly the retail landscape was changing. A few months after that, Lord & Taylor filed for bankruptcy.

Takeaways

AUTHENTICITY MAKES AN IMPRESSION

- **Authenticity isn't just a trait; it's a strategy.**
  When Jim Viola interviewed me, he wasn't looking for another candidate to fill a role. He sought someone capable with depth and passion. Merely reciting my achievements wouldn't have earned me a spot in the training program. To set myself apart, I shared a genuine piece of my journey that resonated with the values and ethos of the company. I didn't craft my story just to impress; it genuinely reflected my character and conveyed the essence of who I am. When used as a guiding principle, authenticity leads to deeper connections, more meaningful engagements, and, ultimately, enduring success.

- **Yesterday is not tomorrow.**
  It's important to treasure our roots, but it's imperative to recalibrate for the future. Lord & Taylor was a hallmark of fashion for discerning young women for more than two centuries. Yet, in modern times, seduced by the allure of expansion, they sacrificed a peerless identity to pursue growth. As they relinquished their distinctive brand essence for scale, they morphed into just another face in the crowd.

Lord & Taylor's storied past should have been the foundation for a vibrant future. The very legacy and authenticity that formed their backbone had the potential to captivate new generations. Leveraging insights from visionary leaders like Dorothy Shaver could have sketched a path to renaissance, but amidst the rapid upheavals of the retail landscape, Lord & Taylor faded into monotony and eventually into the annals of retail history.

- **Don't mortgage the future.**
A legacy isn't built on shortcuts or transient strategies but instead set in the concrete of long-term vision and sustained commitment. A trip to Lord & Taylor was more than a transaction; it was a curated experience. The store embodied elegance, exclusivity, and just what its clientele coveted: the perfect ensemble to elevate special moments.

The relentless pressure of modern business can tempt leaders to chase quick wins. Women didn't flock to Lord & Taylor for bargains, yet tactics like discount coupons can seem clever for short-term sales boosts. Such approaches risk eroding the brand's equity, shifting the narrative from luxury and exclusivity to commoditization and price. Coupons are hardly special. They don't encapsulate what made Lord & Taylor desirable to generations of devoted shoppers.

3. Exceed Expectations

After graduating from the executive training program, I remained posted in women's sportswear, where I had to get used to the rigid hierarchical culture. It was sometimes ruthless and often soulless, but in those days, that was how they raised young sharks to become the predators of tomorrow. One look around the office suggested the method might be working—the baby sharks were learning to swim. And feed—though sometimes on each other.

Was that a good thing? Were we really supposed to be sharks? Why not human beings selling fabulous clothes to other human beings?

I didn't admire the ferociously cutthroat culture or the executives who sustained it, but I didn't question it either. I was determined to fit in and learn. So, I adjusted my expectations, but I vowed to myself that one day, when I was in charge, I would do something to fix how the leaders of tomorrow were trained.

Meanwhile, my job had me running errands. On trips around the store, I'd often wind up in one of the royal elevators with a very senior executive. And every elevator moment shared with a senior leader—and even those not so senior—went the same way. Interaction between the classes seemed designed to be predictable and narrowly focused. The rigid hierarchy was there, always.

"What's selling?" the senior leader would demand while I racked my brain for an answer that would demonstrate my perceptive grasp of the business. I wanted to show them I had useful knowledge to contribute. I wanted to be somebody worth listening to.

One day in a particularly slow selling month, I was returning from Xeroxing our latest sales figures, which were disappointing. I pressed the button for the elevator, and when it opened, I found myself face-to-face with Ms. Bufano, Executive Vice President for *all* of Women's Ready to Wear—my boss's boss's boss.

I almost smiled, but I had absorbed just enough of the culture to know smiling was professionally risky. Smiling implied you weren't serious. Sharks don't smile. So, I nodded an expressionless, silent hello.

"What's selling?" she asked, but I imagined I heard a hint of human warmth in her tone. Had she recognized me as someone from her division?

I decided to respond outside the format, maybe even strike up a conversation based on my up-to-minute knowledge of the sales figures.

"Oof!" I groaned, then offered her a pained, we're-all-in-this-together smile. "Not much, lately."

"That's unfortunate," Ms. Bufano said, exiting the elevator and disappearing into a magnificent wonderland of executive offices.

I felt almost giddy, thinking I might have made an impression on Ms. Bufano. I made my way back to the office with a spring in my step. But the afterglow didn't last. I heard my buyer slam the phone as I walked past her office.

"EVAN!"

I turned into her office and was met with a glare.

"My boss said you told her boss that nothing in our department is selling!"

"Well, I told her it was looking like a tough season. I had the numbers--"

"Are you out of your freakin' mind? Do you know how bad you just made me look? That's my name—*my* name!—on the top of every sales report. This is my department, and anything you do or say reflects on me. Telling Bufano 'Nothing is selling," makes you look like an idiot. And it's not even true. We have a lot of things that are selling—I mean, we do, right? Right?"

Maybe mine wasn't the most strategic answer, but her shouting didn't make it better. A calm explanation of my gaffe was all I needed to ensure it never happened again. Harsh criticism for failing to meet an expectation she never established was not only unkind but also a lesson in destroying morale.

I wanted success. I was not going to let the sharks consume me. I showed up every day ready to perform—actually, out-perform. I was eager to learn.

Unlike the fire department, an assistant buyer's schedule was mostly predictable. On Mondays, every assistant in the buying office did exactly the same thing. We reported to the office by 7:00 a.m. to await delivery of the weekly selling report—several hundred pages of printouts detailing the product sales for each department in the store. The reports recapped the selling prices, profit margins, and remaining inventory.

Each assistant buyer was responsible for digging through the reams of paper to find and collate the information our buyers would need. They depended on us to supply the information essential for their purchasing. And senior management would use the same information to assess each department's performance.

Extracting the relevant sales data from the mass printout was important and dictated many of the week's business activities. Every Monday, we assistants were a flock of sheep, mindlessly hunting down our own numbers in the reams of printer paper, then keying them into spreadsheets while impatient buyers looked over our shoulders.

Despite my executive job title, I was more of a glorified data entry clerk. Every Monday, I sat at the Formica countertop, mindlessly entering numbers into Lotus 1-2-3, the gold standard of spreadsheet programs back then. And every Monday, I felt more frustrated with the tedious time-suck. There had to be a better way of gathering, collating, and distributing crucial sales intel. It was the 20th century! Almost the 21st! Wasn't this the Information Age?

There were about 100 assistant buyers in the company. The average salary was probably $45,000. That's a payroll of roughly $5 million. And we all became data entry clerks every Monday—20% of the week. It cost the company a million dollars a week while our buyers paced impatiently, waiting for crucial data to be sorted, organized, and entered into the system—more wasted time and probably another million in payroll.

Why weren't we receiving the data electronically to sort and collate as needed? Why the extra step, which meant overpaying executives to perform clerical tasks? The standard reports were printouts from a computer. Why not create the summaries everyone needed on the same computer?

This straightforward fix seemed obvious. I suspected the Monday drudgery was drudging on because it was "just how it was done." The people responsible for our "information" systems probably didn't recognize their customers' need for a better product. It's a common scenario in cultures that emphasize individual survival over teamwork. Information gets stored in silos, which limits the cross-functional collaboration that powers successful teams. And a lot of time gets wasted.

Remember the New York City staccato? *Time is money.* From my time in the FD, I knew that anyone could identify problems, but only real leaders have what it takes to drive their teams toward solutions.

It was the mid-1990s. John R. Mashey at Silicon Graphics had just been credited with first using the phrase "Big Data." Database programs were all the rage—yet the brightest programmers often lacked a fundamental understanding of their end users' needs. This was precisely the disconnect at Lord & Taylor.

As it happened, I had become somewhat of a computer nerd during my often quiet nights at the firehouse. I learned to build networks and implemented the first database program to track emergency calls, equipment, and other vital statistics. I wasn't a programmer, but I knew more than anyone else in the buying office at Lord & Taylor, so I became the go-to tech guy.

The bar for being a tech wizard in those days was pretty low. By today's standards, my knowledge of systems architecture and databases was primitive. But I knew enough to hypothesize a solution for our Monday blues.

On my first anniversary at L&T, I had a touch-base meeting with LJ, who had run my executive training class. I admired LJ and thought the feeling was mutual. I considered her a true friend at the company. With LJ, I felt "seen."

She asked how things were going in the buying office. I trusted her, so I decided to be candid. Before long, I was on my soapbox, ranting about the wasted hours preventing me and my cohorts from doing more meaningful work on the business.

At first, LJ seemed taken aback by my questioning of company procedure. However, she also seemed genuinely interested in what I had to say. I told her I wasn't there to dump the Monday problem in her lap. Problems were a dime a dozen. The shortage was in solutions.

I asked her for an introduction to the IT department so I could do some fact-finding. If I could learn how the data was stored, I figured I could work out a solution to the Monday problem.

"Let me do some research, Evan. I'll get back to you soon. I promise."

And the following week, LJ called me to her office. Given the corporate culture, I figured I was in trouble, but what happened next was unexpectedly positive. LJ thanked me for speaking up and offering to find a solution. She told me about the Merchant Task Interference Committee, which aimed to identify and fix inefficiencies in the buying office. She suggested I attend the next meeting as an observer to get a flavor of how the group operated. The committee included some of the highest-level people from the merchandising organization as well as the leaders of the information systems team. These were people way above my pay grade, whom I had never met, but everyone knew who they were. I was thrilled she had followed up with me and excited for the opportunity.

At the first committee meeting I attended, LJ and I took chairs along the wall. It began with two senior vice presidents of merchandising trying to explain a reporting problem to the senior systems team. The systems people just weren't getting it, and as the conversation—actually more like confrontation—picked up steam, both sides became agitated. It was the classic Tower of Babel; neither side spoke the language of the other. They were all top people in their fields of expertise, but their understanding of each other was minimal.

"I still do not understand why you can't produce the report I need!" snarled one of the SVPs.

"The information you want lives in different databases," the senior systems guy replied. "We would need to run an import from multiple SQL Servers, which is possible, but the calculations you want will have to batch process overnight."

The SVP threw up her hands in a gesture of frustration, followed by sighs from everyone on her side of the table. The SVP had no idea what a batch was or why it would take a whole night to process it.

Even the meeting's geography—two teams facing off across a table—seemed a set-up designed for confrontation.

"There has to be a way," the other SVP intervened.

"No way we can meet your deadline," the systems guy insisted. "Can't be done."

And that, apparently, was that.

As much as there was a storm brewing between the two sides in the meeting, a bigger storm was brewing within me. LJ had made it clear that I was there as an observer, but I knew I could help. My mind wrestled with a barrage of questions and doubts. What if my perspective, though born from a lower rank, held merit? Could my intervention steer the conversation towards a more fruitful outcome, or would it be met with disdain or dismissal from stepping out of line?

The idea of voicing my thoughts felt like crossing an invisible line, but remaining silent felt like a betrayal of my convictions. With each passing second, my internal struggle escalated. My heart pounded a mixed drumbeat of anxiety and courage, almost nudging me to speak up with each beat. In that moment of turmoil, where fear and duty waged a silent war, I chose courage and conviction over conformity.

"Excuse me," I said, standing up. "I'm only here to observe, but I have one idea that might deliver what is needed using the existing systems architecture."

The warriors around the table stopped glaring at each other and glared at me.

"I assume you could convert the SQL queries into delimited files?" I asked the systems leader.

"Of course."

From his tone, I think he really wanted to say *Duh*.

"Great. If you create the files and drop them into the Merchant network drive, I can build a macro to import the data, format it, and calculate it for the merchants each week."

"That's all they need?" the systems guy asked, surprised by the simplicity of the solution.

"Yep. I'll set it up from the merchant side and make sure it works for them."

And just like that, I had closed out a stubborn agenda item and pushed the two sides to a peaceful accord.

As I sat down, LJ stood up and said proudly, "Allow me to introduce Evan Dash, one of my Executive Trainees. Evan's now an assistant buyer in Women's Sportswear."

I felt my future in business coming into focus. I was the creative solutions guy who thought outside the box —or the silo, for that matter. I became a permanent member of that committee. My ideas eventually reshaped Mondays for the entire buying team. We ditched a lot of drudgery and gained much-needed productive time. And I had made a name for myself. Literally. Now, when the elevator doors opened, senior leaders said, "Hello, Evan!" instead of "What's selling?"

Takeaways

EXCEED EXPECTATIONS

- **Career advancement lies in exceeding expectations.**
  I realized that career advancement wasn't just about checking boxes but commanding respect and admiration from those around me. The best path forward wasn't just about meeting benchmarks but reducing friction and enhancing experiences. While meeting expectations kept me in the shadows, surpassing them spotlighted me, drawing engagement, trust, and new challenges. Exceeding expectations made me appear more capable and stand out, and standing out fuels career success.

- **Earn a reputation as a problem solver.**
  The best way to make an indelible mark is to locate and solve problems. The FD taught me, "Where there's smoke, there's fire." In business, this translates to "Where there are frustrations, there are opportunities." Frustration is the best indicator of a problem in need of a solution. By discussing the solution for a specific pain point with LJ, I unknowingly set the stage for a turning point in my career. If I didn't speak up in the room of senior leaders, my career at Lord & Taylor might have continued on its dispiriting trajectory from frustration to disengagement to resignation. Instead, knowing I had something worthwhile to say, I spoke up and exceeded everyone's expectations. This wasn't just another day at work; it was the day I came into my own at Lord & Taylor.

4. People Make the Difference

As a kid, I woke early each morning to watch my father perform his pre-dawn ritual. With purposeful movements, he would button his dress shirt, twist his tie into a perfect knot, put on his suit, and smooth the fabric in the mirror. His look was modern-day gladiator: sharp and powerful with broad shoulders—a commanding presence.

He would kiss Mom and me goodbye and then catch a crowded commuter train for New York City. Most of the men on that train were dressed very much like my dad. His suit and tie were more than a fashion statement; it was the uniform of the white-collar American executive or professional in pursuit of the American Dream.

During my high school years in the 1980s, commuting fathers rarely attended after-school sporting events. Yet my dad, somehow, arrived just in time for every one of my games. He would stand next to the bleachers; he never sat down. And how he dressed—smart suit, perfectly knotted tie—symbolized his dedication—not just to his career, but to his family.

When my dad began his work life, it must have seemed unlikely that he would ever own a suit, much less wear one every weekday. Born in the Bronx, he started working as an auto mechanic at age 16, pursuing an honest, blue-collar future. For extra money, he worked as a stock boy in a retail store. When his boss asked him to change lightbulbs in the store, he jumped into the task. Always one to go the extra mile, perched on the scaffolding, he took the initiative and cleaned years of dust from the ceiling. A regional manager noticed and gave him more stores to maintain before formally offering him a path to a retail career.

My dad had grit and determination. He became the president of Fan Club, an athletic footwear retail chain, and later, vice chairman of Marshalls. Standing tall, with perfect posture, he looked the part. His suit and tie were all business; this was not a man to be trifled with. My dad always stood out in a crowd. At my basketball games, I could hear his large hands clapping thunderously whenever I made a shot.

At the time, I didn't grasp what a feat it was for him to make it to my games. Unlike many other suburban dads in suits riding those commuter trains, mine had figured out a work-life balance. His career was important. His family was more important. I think he got that right—and set a great example.

As baby boomers dug into their careers, many tried to figure out that *work vs. life* issue. The clothes people wore to work were the first signal that things were changing.

Casual Fridays began in Hawaii as "Aloha Friday," a garment trade promotion encouraging men to wear Hawaiian shirts one day a week to support the local textile industry. The idea caught on in California and spread across the country. When Casual Friday hit the mainstream, it was more than a change in fashion—it was a shift in the American lifestyle. Baby boomers were questioning the rigid line separating work-life and life-life. *Casual Fridays* were a symbol and symptom of a significant cultural shift.

By the end of my first year at Lord & Taylor, I had hit my stride and gained confidence. I was blissfully unaware of our collision course with Casual Fridays until a young leader took me under his wing and taught me the importance of staying aware of cultural changes. Sooner or later, these changes always worked their way into the retail world.

Around my one-year milestone at Lord & Taylor, I was reassigned to Menswear—specifically, Men's Suits, the symbol of sartorial tyranny many men at the time were ditching. Casual Fridays had soon spilled over into slightly less casual Thursdays. Even Mondays were starting to look more relaxed too. Great for people, but not so good for the Men's Suits business.

After swimming in the shark tank that was Women's Sportswear, my expectations for Menswear were low, especially given the devastation of the suit business. Filled with apprehension, I reported to Menswear early Monday morning. Their offices were in an adjacent building, with an employee entrance I had never used.

Right away, Menswear felt like a different company. Vibrant décor adorned the walls. Music was playing. A group of interesting-looking people gathered outside one cubicle, talking casually and even laughing. Laughter was a high crime in Women's Sportswear.

Still, there was no denying the dark clouds on the Menswear horizon. The clouds were already overhead and raining on our parade. Casual Fridays had done a serious number on suit sales. That business had come to a grinding halt. I figured I might be out of a job even before getting my feet wet.

Sir Isaac Newton's third law of motion states that "every action has an equal and opposite reaction." This usually holds true in retail, so someone would benefit from the menswear implosion. As men shunned suits for more casual attire, the beneficiary at L&T was Glenn Robinson, my counterpart in the Sport Coat and Blazer department.

Blazers had, well, caught fire.

Glenn and I reported to Jeff Moore, a young and even-keeled Vice President and the most adept problem-solver I had ever met.

Changing departments, I had already experienced a radical shift in workplace culture. Instead of gunning for each other, people boosted and supported their peers. Our boss asked questions and listened to what we had to say. There was no blaming or berating—only productive dialogue salted with wry humor, focused on getting the best results. The hierarchy was almost flat. Jeff was a natural-born leader and felt no need to be a tyrant. And despite the challenges in the business, he was a great motivator and a superb coach who instilled a winning spirit in the team. Coming out of our meetings, I always felt energized, ready to take on the problems we were facing, and prepared to meet the challenges. And I knew Jeff had my back.

My suit business was shrinking while Glenn's sport coat business was doubling. But while we focused on our respective businesses, Jeff saw the bigger picture. Glenn and I each had specific, self-serving plans for our own floor space, but Jeff's perspective was more dynamic and agile. To Jeff, space was space, and yesterday's thinking was irrelevant. The future was all that mattered. Seventy percent of the selling floor was dedicated to suits, but right now, sport coats needed the acreage—and no whining!

Jeff's vision wasn't just about carrying more sport coats; he envisioned us becoming the best sport coat destination in the country. The casual menswear business was about to take off; its energy wouldn't be denied. We could either waste time struggling to catch the horse and lead it back into the barn—or throw a saddle on and ride it. So, with a goal of exponential sport coat growth within 18 months, we were tasked to think strategically and redeploy our resources. Jeff cut my suit space in half and slid the real estate over to Glenn. With the reduction in floor space, my suit inventory would carry us through the remainder of the year, so I didn't have much buying to do. Instead of me sitting around and watching the sport coat business take off, Jeff shifted our responsibilities and assigned me to buy the "blazers" category within the sport coat department.

Jeff had an insatiable curiosity about the world around him. He was determined to adapt his business to the changes unfolding around us. He'd recognized that Casual Friday was more than a weekly chance to wear colorful shirts. It had caught something in the broader culture and was just the beginning of a lasting change in men's fashion.

Under his leadership, we transformed a potential menswear calamity into a colossal success. Within a year, the combined revenue of the suit and sport coat departments posted the largest increase that anyone at Lord & Taylor could recall.

Jeff taught me thought leadership—paying attention to changes working their way through the cultures. Accepting what was beyond my control and staying nimble enough to capitalize on change was vital. He wanted his teams lithe and agile, responding quickly to changes on the field —not locked into some outdated old game plan.

Had Jeff approached our predicament with the tunnel vision common to most retailers, sales would have tanked, and he would have—correctly—blamed it on the rise of Casual Fridays, just as I was prepared to do. Instead, like a hockey player who anticipates where the puck is headed, Jeff saw the game shifting before him and took swift action to position our business to where the puck—in this case, the consumer— was going. His big-picture perspective and ability to lead his team to swift and effective actions changed the game. Jeff's plan made Glenn and me look great. And instead of doing the sharks-eats-shark, me-me-me thing, Jeff gave us credit for the results.

After I'd been in Menswear for six months, I was promoted and became the buyer of sport coats and dress pants. Jeff's confidence in my ability allowed me to skip the level of associate buyer.

It is uncommon for anyone at Jeff's level to take a chance on a young executive. But he took the time and trouble to know his people and was confident I was worth the risk. He recognized that I took on every task, delivered my best, and never complained. I was determined to succeed. Jeff respected that.

As I adjusted to my new role, I discovered that my expectations didn't entirely align with the reality of the job. The buyers I worked for seemed empowered to make all decisions for their departments. I'd failed to recognize that, while they may have had the freedom to choose the product styles and colors, all significant decisions—selection of suppliers, pricing, and advertising of products —were made by those higher up.

Rather than running my department, it felt like my real role was to assist Jeff at the drop of a hat. He would often pull me away from my department to focus on a problem critical to him.

I tried to conceal my frustration until one day, I couldn't. I had been abruptly summoned to Jeff's office and handed yet another emergency assignment.

"You can handle this, Evan, right? Shouldn't take long, but stay on it for as long as it takes."

I gave him a death stare.

"Problem?" Jeff asked.

Problem? I'd just been pulled away from a stack of problems. Problems were piled on my desk.

"There are a couple of things I'm in the middle of," I snarled. "But, you know, whatever."

"You seem frustrated," he said calmly. "Tell me about it."

His calm demeanor immediately diffused my anger. I tried to speak honestly, without resentment, *sans* whining.

"I worked very hard as an assistant. I assumed that once I was promoted, I'd control my time. But I feel like I'm an assistant again. I mean, *your* assistant."

"Don't get me wrong, Jeff, I'm grateful you took a chance on me. I guess I just expected my days would be mine to control. I have responsibilities, and I need to be able to deal with them."

Jeff smiled. "Everyone is someone's assistant, Evan. When I ask you to do something for me," he said, "it's because my boss asked me to do it for her. I need you to assist me as I assist her. I get it. It's hard sometimes, but those are the rules of the game."

He let his words sink in. Whenever I spoke with Jeff, the bigger picture always came into focus. That was his gift. He empathized with me because he was experiencing the same frustration I was experiencing. Empathy made me respond in kind. From then on, whenever he asked for my help, I gladly dropped what I was doing to help him deal with the problem or project of the moment. I recognized it was an essential part of my job—not a distraction from my job.

That breakthrough moment in Jeff's office was the first time I felt the type of camaraderie that we had counted on in the fire department. Jeff's empathy was transformative. It shifted my entire approach toward my job. I became the go-to guy on Jeff's team, as Jeff was a go-to guy for the company.

People refer to a company as a living, breathing entity, but a company is just the people who work there, and they can make it into anything they want it to be. Sure, the standards are set by senior leadership, but the individuals throughout the organization create the overall atmosphere.

Influential leaders not only set clear direction, they also cultivate a culture of shared beliefs and values. Inspired leaders foster an environment of empathy and camaraderie and build these into the DNA of their businesses.

Frustration, malaise, and apathy can also get ingrained in a company's ethos. This is why leaders must make sure the positive values are understood, embraced, and lived every day by everyone in the company and that the leaders practice what they preach.

Outstanding leaders like Jeff lead by example, not by mission statements or press releases. They know their actions speak louder than words.

When I started at Lord & Taylor, I witnessed co-workers —men and women—mistreated, overlooked, demeaned, and marginalized. The culture was cold and cutthroat. When I moved to Menswear, I experienced a whole different culture within the same company. Suddenly, I was working in a phenomenal organization that prioritized its employees. The job responsibilities and top management's guidance remained the same, but the people I met and the examples they set were in total contrast to the shark-fest that was women's sportswear.

I looked to the future with excitement, knowing that as my career developed, I would have the power to influence and maybe shape the culture in my workplace. My actions and choices, my respect for others, and my sense of the team could boost the morale of those around me and improve the quality of our collective work. There was no reason to accept swimming in a shark tank when I could contribute to a challenging, forward-thinking environment that empowers people to do great work and develop their careers. I was ready to move forward with the knowledge and confidence that it was incumbent on me to make things happen.

Takeaways

PEOPLE MAKE THE DIFFERENCE

- **Behind a great culture lies vision and empathy.**
  My best and worst jobs were both within the same company, underscoring that people shape the character of a workplace. In womenswear, the people proved how quickly leadership without empathy can undermine a workplace culture. Jeff, on the other hand, embodied empathetic leadership. Operating within a broader corporate framework with challenges, he managed to carve out an oasis of motivation and innovation. He recognized that a thriving workplace needs more than mantras from the executive suite. Jeff didn't tell us how to act—he showed us. He was unambiguous about our values and expected every team member to embody them. When you lead by example, you don't create followers; you create the next leaders.

- **Empathy increases motivation.**
  My journey with Jeff was transformative. He mentored and promoted me to buyer before I met the qualifications because he believed in me. I reciprocated with a deep sense of loyalty and commitment. Jeff never lost touch with those beneath him on the corporate ladder, so he was generous with success. When he drew praise from around the company, he'd let us know, which motivated us even more.

- **It's better to be a thought leader than a victim**
  Jeff epitomized this philosophy. Always attuned to the business landscape, he embraced change, seeing it not as a threat but as a hidden opportunity. This agility in his thinking allowed us to take decisive actions when we needed to change with the times. Jeff's ability to anticipate, not just react, ensured that we aligned our offerings to where the customers were going, not where they had been.

- **Family matters.**
  My dad showed me the importance of work-life balance. I'll never forget the feeling of having him show up at my games when he "should have been" at work. Years later, I followed in his footsteps, sharing in the excitement of my own sons' after-school achievements—like Daniel's first slam dunk and Charlie's undefeated tennis season. I'll delve deeper into how I shaped a more modern philosophy for achieving work-life harmony in Chapter 21.

- **Don't wait for luck to strike.**
  My father did right by people and went above and beyond. When he fixed cars, he did it honestly. When assigned to change lightbulbs in a retail store, he went the extra mile and cleaned the ceilings. People took notice, which opened the door to a successful career in retail. A great work ethic and doing right by others always creates more opportunities than luck does. Odds are, you'll find these traits in people who seem to be "lucky" all the time.

5. Every Day is a Job Interview

Life was going well in Menswear. Co-workers would come and go, but I had no interest in leaving. To be a buyer at Lord & Taylor meant something.

When my old friend LJ told me she was leaving for a bigger job at Macy's, I was sad to see her go. On her last day, a group of us took her out for drinks. Before we parted company that night, she took me aside and gave me what I thought would be her last piece of professional advice.

"You have a bright future here," LJ said. "Other companies will try to lure you away. Don't be tempted!"

Why did she sound so emphatic? I reassured her that I wasn't going anywhere.

Exactly one month later, I learned what was behind her cryptic tip. Revelation came in the form of a phone call. I was in my cubicle when the phone buzzed.

"Hello, Mens-"

"Evan, don't say a thing," a familiar voice whispered. "It's LJ. Is anyone around you? Can you talk?"

"Yes. No. I can talk."

Why was I whispering? Somehow, I was already feeling, instantly, conspiratorial.

"I have your next job," LJ said.

It was the last thing I expected to hear, especially from the person who had warned me against leaving Lord & Taylor. Was this some kind of test?

"No way, LJ," I said. "I'm not leaving here to be a buyer at Macy's."

"Oh, give me more credit than that, Evan."

I could almost see her rolling her eyes.

"Evan, I've designed the perfect job for you. You're going to be our Vice President of Strategic Planning."

I was speechless. And LJ had spoken like it was a done deal, all but for the paperwork.

"I need you here tomorrow to meet a few people," she said. "So I can put together the formal offer."

"Tomorrow? Saturday?" I was confused. In shock, actually.

"It's the only time I could get with the CFO, president, and CEO," LJ explained. "It's herding cats. These guys are booked solid. Can you make tomorrow work?"

"Sure. Yeah. Yes. Of course."

At Lord & Taylor, I had met the CEO only that one time in LJ's exec training class. I didn't even know who our CFO was.

"It's just a formality. This job is made for you. I told them about your great work, and they're excited to meet you."

"I'll be there," I promised. "And LJ? Wow. Thank you. Thanks for looking out for me."

When I hung up, I realized LJ had plans for me even before she started at Macy's. My time with her on the tech committee had been like a job interview, allowing me to showcase my unique talents. LJ had watched me exercising skills in negotiation, persuasion, and problem-solving. Skills she hadn't known I possessed until then but were perfectly matched to a job that didn't even exist —until she created it.

The job sounded like a perfect fit, but I was having a hard time believing that Macy's would offer a vice president position to a 25-year-old. VPs were typically 40-something, long in experience, with impressive track records. I tried not to get my hopes up, but I was practically jumping out of my skin over the opportunity.

I met LJ at her new office bright and early Saturday morning. She prepped me for the meetings, leaving nothing to chance, making sure I understood the expectations of the people I was about to meet.

"You think these guys would take a chance on someone young like me?"

LJ dismissed my concerns with a nonchalant wave of her hand. "Look, Evan, the future is all about innovation and technology. Youth is an advantage, so believe me, your strengths are exactly what this place needs right now, so get your game face on."

As LJ led me into the executive suite, I gaped at the palatial, over-the-top décor of the place. I felt like a peasant who had wandered into the Halls of Versailles. Golden sconces punctuated a long, wide corridor hung with portraits of Macy's past presidents and chairmen. They reminded me of the paintings of ancient kings I had encountered on Sunday visits to the Metropolitan Museum.

Dark floorboards were covered with Persian rugs, a perfect complement to the deep red walls and mahogany wainscoting. We walked to the end of the long hallway and stopped in the waiting area of the president's office.

"Wait here," LJ said, gesturing toward an elegant, ornate sofa. "I'll see if he's ready for you."

I nodded, sat down, and settled into the sofa to wait for my cue. I was trying to beat back the butterflies to no avail. I found myself staring at one portrait, one ancient face. Something about it was mesmerizing. I stood up and approached the painting. The colors were dark and somber, which made the distressed gold frame gleam by contrast.

The old man in the portrait was mostly bald but with a full gray beard. A wise man, an elder. A man who knew himself. Willful. Mindful. Aware.

"That's Isidor Straus," said a voice behind me, startling me out of my trance. I turned to find LJ and a distinguished looking older gentleman standing behind me.

"This is James Gray," LJ said, "President of Macy's. Mr. Gray, this is Evan Dash, the young man I've been telling you about."

Mr. Gray shook my hand and smiled warmly.

"I'll leave you two to get acquainted," LJ said and disappeared.

Mr. Gray and I stood and looked at the portrait together.

"It's a powerful portrait," I said, feeling that I needed to communicate what I had felt. "I almost expected him to walk off the wall and talk to me."

Mr. Gray smiled. "Isidor Straus was the co-owner of Macy's in the late 1800s. He and his brother started it all with a crockery department in the basement, and he wound up owning the whole thing. He had a good run with this place until he and his wife died together on the deck of the Titanic. Ida refused to get in the lifeboat. She gave their maid her fur coat and told her to get into the boat in her place. She didn't want to leave Isidor. My definition of true love," Mr. Gray said.

He motioned for me to follow him back to his office.

We sat down to talk, and I got a good look at Mr. Gray. He was in his sixties, with an easy smile that made him seem genuine and warm.

He began telling me how he felt about Macy's. I could tell he was a true believer. He told me Macy's was woven into the very fabric of American culture. He loved the Thanksgiving Day Parade. He loved coming to work every day and being surrounded by hard-working, intelligent people.

I had anticipated a tough, take-no-prisoners interview, but Mr. Gray spent about half an hour selling *ME* on the company. He was graceful, genuine, and calm—a true Southern gentleman. He was also brilliant. We talked about the technology reshaping the retail universe, and in my youthful hubris, I was impressed that someone so much older had such a vivid understanding of technological progress. He had all kinds of charts and data and plenty of genuine enthusiasm for the projects I would focus on.

Time flew. I had been there for over an hour when LJ knocked on the door.

"Thank you, LJ, for introducing us," Mr. Gray said. He stood up and came around his desk, and we shook hands.

"Very stimulating conversation, Evan. We probably could have talked all day. Energy and ideas are exactly what we need. I look forward to working with you."

"Me as well, Mr. Gray," I said.

He held up his finger. "Please. It's Jim".

"Okay, Jim," I said. Then I turned and followed LJ out the door. I wanted to pinch myself as she walked me down the hall to my next meeting. I knew I was in.

After four hours of back-to-back interviews—which felt more like conversations among peers—LJ parked me in the Executive Boardroom.

It was almost three decades ago, but I remember it like yesterday. The enormous leather chairs were, presumably, built for people much more important than me. There were 24 of them around a gigantic table that must have been swung in by a crane. I sat alone for at least half an hour, buzzing with anticipation. Minutes passed like hours.

At last, one of the double doors swung open, and LJ walked in with Lawrence Anderson, Executive Vice President of Planning. Lawrence and I had hit it off earlier, and I was already calling him Larry. He was there to make me a formal offer.

He sat down next to me and spread some papers on the table. The first page was a formal offer letter for the vice president of strategic planning. The salary was more than double my current buyer's salary, the signing bonus was beyond sweet, and there were all sorts of additional perks.

But the opportunity wasn't the title, the salary, or any of the enticements in that set of papers. The opportunity was the people. It was the chance to attend the Harvard of retail, experience many more days like this one, and learn from some of the most intelligent, creative people I had ever encountered. The biggest brains of retail. Men and women whose portraits would one day line these walls, enshrined in Macy's history as a reward for their skillful stewardship of the company.

I looked across the table to LJ and smiled, then turned to Larry and told him I was all in.

When opportunity knocks, you open the door.

Takeaways

EVERY DAY IS A JOB INTERVIEW

- **Today's hustle becomes tomorrow's highlight.**
  I used to think that job interviews were where opportunities were created. However, when LJ called me about Macy's, I realized that transformative opportunities spring from our daily actions, like staying late to finish an assignment, helping a struggling colleague, or showing leadership on a committee. With every initiative you undertake, every solution you propose, and every challenge you navigate, you're showcasing your skills, ambition, integrity, and potential—often to people who can advance your career. Most managers prefer to hire someone endorsed by a trusted associate over a pile of "qualified candidates." When LJ raved to the top leadership about my work at Lord & Taylor, they never considered the stack of resumes. After observing my performance over the previous year, LJ had already sealed my next offer.

- **See the person behind the title.**
  As a firefighter, I helped all kinds of people. Emergencies are a great leveler. In the heat of crisis, status distinctions fade; the CEO and the factory worker stand on equal ground, both equally deserving of assistance and compassion. The ability to connect, human to human, becomes paramount.

In the corporate world, titles often mask the people behind them, preventing genuine connections. Serving on the technology committee redefined my perspective. When the top leaders saw the value I added, it boosted my confidence, taking me back to my FD days, which melted away their titles. My ability to connect as people instead of playing my role in the hierarchy was instrumental in my corporate success. The human connections I made at Macy's helped seal my new position.

6. Storytelling and Seafood

Macy's had a jingle in the 1970s, *'Macy's. We're a part of your life.'* It was only a tagline—but it meant something special to me. Macy's *has been* a part of my life since first grade when I made my first TV appearance. There I was, riding the turkey float on Thanksgiving Day, holding my little brother, Matthew, by the hand, waving to the television cameras in Herald Square as Donny Osmond belted out *Give My Regards to Broadway.*

Long before the retail giant recruited me, my father worked for Macy's. Some of my earliest memories are riding those old wooden escalators down to the Macy's Cellar with my dad. The rush of the city, the scents and sounds, the sparkle and glamour of beautiful things—I experienced the world's largest store as an exciting field trip.

Twenty years later, walking into Macy's as a newly minted vice president felt surreal. I settled into a corner office with a sweeping view of Madison Square Garden and a painting of Herald Square on the wall. *This,* I thought, *this is big time.*

Like Lord & Taylor, Macy's began on Manhattan's Lower East Side almost two centuries ago. Unlike Lord & Taylor,

Macy's was not a fashion-forward leader for New Yorkers of a certain class. Macy's went for mass appeal, selling almost everything to nearly everyone.

Right from the start, Macy's created newsworthy moments. Back then, news was the only thing that traveled across the nation. In 1904, Macy's relocated to Herald Square to become *The Largest Store in The World*. They gobbled up an entire city block—24 acres of shopping space. They invited the Strauss Brothers to open a China Department in their basement, instantly creating the first department store. This too, was news. Then, they began an annual Christmas parade using animals from the Central Park Zoo and got national headlines. Same with the fireworks display on the Fourth of July. Then *Miracle on 34th Street* established Macy's as Santa's pied-à-terre in New York City for movie audiences across America. Like Mr. Gray told me, a company woven into the country's culture.

From the outset, Macy's built their brand on masterful storytelling. By the early 1900s, Macy's was already creating newsworthy selfie moments. That's why they did the parades and the fireworks and stayed open until midnight on Christmas Eve—and that's why they invented Black Friday. These events became widely shared stories woven into the fabric of American culture long before anyone dreamed of social media. I knew Macy's was going to be a tremendously exciting, fulfilling place to work.

They had hired me to "implement cutting-edge technology to deliver better retail results." My team would be among the first to leverage big data to stay competitive in a retail future that would become definitively digital. So, no more bulky black binders crammed with out-of-date reports. We would make the sea of data work for us, not drown us.

There was a generation gap to bridge. Many retail elders viewed computers as unnecessary, even sinister contraptions that redacted the human element from their jobs. Meanwhile, the younger generation had to navigate a flood of information that was suddenly and overwhelmingly available to extract what actually mattered.

Inspired by Macy's storytelling heritage, I immediately looked for the stories our data was telling. Once I knew the story, I could create strategies to improve sales and profit.

My first assignment was an issue with Liz Claiborne activewear, where we had accumulated an unexpected excess of merchandise in our clearance section. I began with a small experiment and selected a group of stores across the Tri-state area. Then, I dissected the sales figures to the lowest level—by size and store location for each item. Finally, I visited these stores to observe the customer shopping patterns and combined my observations and the data to reveal the underlying story.

In one suburban store in South Jersey, women were buying Liz Claiborne predominantly in larger sizes, leaving the smaller sizes for clearance. In Queens, though, they sold out of the smaller sizes while the larger ones moved to the clearance rack. If we had stocked more suitable sizes by store, we could have sold 30 percent more merchandise at full price and satisfied more customers. With the story revealed, the solution was obvious. I would work with our buyers and the supplier to get the right sizes into the right stores from the outset, which wouldn't take much convincing. With some simple charts and a financial model showing sales and profits way above plan, it was a no-brainer for the buyers to give it a shot. And soon, they were glad they did.

My immediate boss was Lawrence E. Anderson, the man who had hired me. Like Jim Gray, who seemed to be channeling the enterprising spirit of Isadore Strauss, Larry connected with Macy's populist soul. He knew that their great stories grabbed attention, inspired loyalty, and kept Macy's front and center in the retail world.

Larry also knew a lot about life. He saw leadership lessons in everything and passed them along in stories from his past, most of which had nothing to do with Macy's. And yet they had everything to do with being a respected retailer, a strong leader, and a good person.

In all my previous jobs, I sat close to my bosses, who literally supervised me all day. Guidance was given in real-time, all day, every day, whether it was needed or not. Larry's style was different. I only saw him at our weekly update meetings. He didn't check up on me. He never stopped by my office. I don't think he even knew where my office was. His hands-off approach wasn't disinterest; it reflected satisfaction. He was happy with my work and saw no need to over-manage me.

Instead, he used our weekly updates to coach and mentor me in areas where I wasn't as strong—management skills in particular. Each week, he touched on a different aspect of leadership, helping me to see my role in the bigger picture.

During one meeting, I complained about having to depend on people who didn't report to me or respect my deadlines, which often left me frantically scrambling to complete my own work on time. As I whined, Larry reclined in his chair and smiled. He let me finish. Then, he had a story to tell.

"Back in the day," he told me, "I was maître d' at a popular restaurant in Cape Cod. The owner counted on the summer months to make his profit for the whole year. To maximize profits, he understaffed and overbooked—a bad combination for hungry customers or servers surviving on tips.

"It ruined the dining-out experience for everyone. It worked for the owner, though. It was August in Cape Cod, and he knew people would wait and buy drinks at the bar before finally getting their table. But nobody was leaving happy or satisfied, and the whole situation stressed me out."

"I felt responsible," Larry said. "I'd watch couples waiting in the bar, getting impatient, getting hungry, starting to get upset. Arguing. What should have been a nice summer evening on the Cape turned tense and edgy because the owner put profits above his customers."

"Then," Larry shrugged, "if they hadn't walked out, they were often ignored after I finally sat them. The servers were doing their best, but understaffed is understaffed. I watched it play out night after night until I realized how to ease the burden on everyone."

I loved Larry's stories. They always somehow connected to a problem or situation I was experiencing, but this time, I wasn't sure where he was going.

"So, what did you do?"

"Okay. So, when guests arrived, I would tell them, 'Sorry, but we are running a little behind tonight. I'm waiting for your table to clear, and the second it does, I'll come to get you.'"

"Then, every 10 minutes or so, I'd go into the bar to let them know I hadn't forgotten about them. As long as they knew I was looking out for them, the upset-impatient-hungry-angry cycle never started. They knew I was caring for them so they could relax in the bar and enjoy a drink or two. Why not? It was a beautiful summer evening; it was Cape Cod, and they were on vacation."

"When I'd finally seat them, I always thanked them for their patience, brought menus, and told them about the specials. I never let them feel neglected or ignored. They could see I cared, and that's all it took. They were happy, I was happy, the servers were happy. Even the owner was happy, and all it cost was a few minutes of extra care and attention at the right time."

"Brilliant! They were still getting lousy service, but you created the illusion of progress. People could even have a good time as long as they knew they weren't forgotten."

Larry smiled. "Those deadlines you're setting for yourself. Those are arbitrary. The people waiting for your material would be fine waiting another week if you kept them in the loop. Check in with them a few days before the deadline to let them know progress is happening, and they'll get great information as soon the work is complete."

"And actually, the delay allows you more opportunities to stay in touch with key people in the company. You pay attention to them, keep them posted, and share your excitement about progress. If they see that you are on it, they'll forget about the deadline, but they'll remember that you were attentive to their needs and the caliber of your work was excellent. It's all about managing expectations."

Larry was right. Managing expectations puts you in control. The alternative was performing a high-pressure rush job, turning in mediocre work, or silently missing deadlines. No matter the outcome, you'll likely make a poor showing. But by being proactive and controlling expectations, you're perfectly positioned to exceed them.

People need to know that you care about them and what *they* care about. Leaders, CEOs, and people vacationing on the Cape all crave the same thing—to feel seen and appreciated.

Larry's lesson helped me to turn my biggest frustration into an opportunity. By showing empathy, I could control expectations, build stronger relationships, and paint myself in the best possible light.

Takeaways

STORYTELLING AND SEAFOOD

- **Craft narratives that resonate.**
  Before there was social media, Macy's tapped into the power of storytelling. By creating newsworthy events, they captured the imaginations and hearts of people across the country. People harbored dreams of a visit even when there wasn't a Macy's for hundreds of miles. This emotional connection made the flagship store in Herald Square a must-visit for both tourists and locals, setting the gold standard for retail therapy.

  Today, our devices bombard us with updates and alerts, overwhelming rather than informing us. But Larry demonstrated that engaging stories land messages, resonating far deeper than an avalanche of information. Authentic stories were his method to engage because great stories hook the audience. Memorable tales, be it Macy's heartwarming 'Miracle on 34th Street,' Disney's Century of Enchantment, or Nike's empowering "Just Do It" campaign, forge lasting emotional bonds. Reflect on your favorite brands; you'll likely find your connection in their stories.

- **Control what you can control.**
  Larry had zero control over inadequate staffing and overbooked reservations, but he refused to be a victim of poor decisions made above his pay grade.

Instead, he figured out what he could control, and by adeptly managing expectations, he went from being overwhelmed to orchestrating memorable experiences. Even though he was working harder, his stress went way down while job satisfaction went way up.

- **Discover what they really want.**
Businesses often misjudge the true needs of their customers. Larry was astute. He realized his patrons just wanted a night out where they felt appreciated and cared for. The extra wait was no big deal once they knew that a thoughtful, attentive person was looking out for them. That summer on Cape Cod, Larry grasped something that many companies forget. By being empathetic to your customers, you win their loyalty in return.

- **Cater to the unique needs of each person.**
Larry understood that I didn't need a supervisor looking over my shoulder. He saw I needed opportunities to develop my abilities as a manager. So, he steered me towards significant strides in management rather than incremental improvements in my daily work.

7. Respect

In my first two weeks at Macy's, I met one-on-one with almost every member of senior management. I wanted to introduce my initiative and enlist their support.

I was able to book appointments with every executive vice president and senior vice president, except one: Anthony Graziosi, Senior Vice President of Home Products. My team would be looking closely at one of Mr. Graziosi's product areas, so it seemed essential to introduce myself and solicit his support.

I kept checking in with his assistant, May, but a month had passed before Mr. Graziosi found the time to see me.

Finally, the big day came. It surprised me that his office was in the back wing of the 15th floor, not along the stately hallway where other senior execs were situated. The rear wing was dingy—a completely different vibe than the executive floor.

May looked up from her desk in the tiny reception area. "Mr. Dash?"

"That's me."

"Mr. Graziosi is running a little behind schedule. Please have a seat. We're having a hectic day."

"Evan," I said.

"Excuse me?"

"Evan. My name. Evan Dash."

"I'm very pleased to meet you, Mr. Dash."

"We've spoken on the phone several times."

"Of course. And Mr. Graziosi is looking forward to meeting you."

"He's a busy guy."

"He certainly is."

No matter how I tried to strike up a conversation, May wanted no part of it, so I sat on one of two dumpy visitor chairs. There were no 19th-century portraits of merchant princes in gilded frames, only holes where pictures had once hung. No Persian rugs, either. Industrial carpet, thin and stained. It was like a waiting area at the Department of Motor Vehicles.

From the inner office, I could hear a deep, gravelly voice with a thick Brooklyn accent yelling on the phone. "Listen, Jay! You come through on your end, or we're gonna have a problem."

Mr. Graziosi certainly sounded like a very direct person. Maybe a little hostile? More like a guy you sent to collect on a debt than a senior vice president of a Fortune 500 company.

I heard him bang down the phone and thought May would escort me in. But no. He immediately got into another call. And another. I'd been there for 30 minutes when a group of people, probably buyers and assistants, arrived. They clustered around May's desk, whispering anxiously until Mr. Graziosi shouted for them. May nodded, and they all entered the inner sanctum in one bunch, like herd animals seeking protection in numbers.

I was in disbelief until the anger bubbling inside of me took over. I'd had enough and stood up. "Are you sure I'm on Tony's calendar, May? I had us down for one o'clock. It's after one-thirty."

May smiled brightly. "We haven't forgotten you, Mr. Dash. We're just terribly busy."

She returned to her computer, and I sat down and scribbled some memos on my Palm Pilot. At least my state-of-the-art handheld day planner allowed me to get some work done, but it was a small consolation compared to the disrespect I felt.

Their meeting wrapped up eventually and the group hustled from Graziosi's office, the last one out firmly closing his door.

Maybe May caught me glancing at my watch. By then, I'd been waiting for an hour and a half. She whispered into her phone, then floated me another bright smile.

"He will see you now, Mr. Dash."

She stood up and opened the door, and there he was—jet-black hair slicked back, dark eyes, leaning back in his black leather office chair on the phone. He had removed his shoes, and his sock-clad feet were parked on his desk.

The office was old-school retail trade: small and plain. It probably hadn't been redecorated in 30 years. My dad's office was something like that—just one picture hung—a baby in a highchair with a bowl of spaghetti dumped on his head and the words, "Why Me."

Tony briefly covered the receiver with his hand and snarled, "Siddown!"

When I took a seat, his feet were practically in my face. So, I shifted to the other visitor's chair, a few inches further from his socks. He was holding the receiver in the crook of his shoulder and clipping his fingernails. I wondered if I was being pranked and looked around for a hidden camera. What next? Would he be taking off the socks and starting on his toenails?

Finally, he slammed down the phone and looked at me directly. Not a welcoming vibe.

"What can I do for you."

It sounded more like an accusation than a question. Clearly, my presence was a waste of his time.

"Thank you for meeting with me, Mr. Graziosi. I'm Evan Dash. I'm the new Vice President of Strategic Planning."

"Good for you. What's that got to do with me?"

Okay, no point making small talk with this guy, so I plunged right in.

"I'm meeting with all the Senior Executives to discuss a new initiative I'm heading. We are focusing on improving inventory management. Our preliminary analysis suggests we can run with less inventory and execute faster turns, driving a new KPI we are tracking called ROGI. It stands for Return on Gross--"

"Who the fuck do you think you are," Tony said sternly.

"Uh, I'm Evan Dash. I'm heading up--"

He swung his feet off the desk, leaned forward in his chair, slammed his nail clipper on the desk, and looked me right in the eyes. I thought for a moment that he would reach across the desk and grab me.

"Do you realize I got more retail knowledge in my fingernail than you have in your whole body?" he said calmly.

Was this a rhetorical question? Was I expected to answer? Uncomfortable silence.

"When you can teach me something about my business, I'll talk to you. Until then, stay the fuck out of my business."

Then he spun his chair around so he didn't have to look at me as though my presence was too gross an insult. And that's when May magically appeared to escort me out. The two of them had a real routine going. Good cop, bad cop? Perfectly choreographed.

I think they enjoyed it. I certainly didn't.

As I retreated to my office, there was a palpable shrinking sensation, a feeling of being diminished. Besides the obvious embarrassment, I was also confused. I struggled to process the words hurled at me, trying to find constructive criticism in what felt like a personal attack.

When things don't go as planned, I try to step back and look at the situation from all sides, a strategy my father taught me. He was always Mr. 360, challenging my position in any argument and testing whether I built my opinions and convictions on a solid foundation.

I tried to see what had just happened from Tony's point of view. He was a busy leader who had been in the business longer than I'd been alive. He led a young buying staff and had a lot on his plate—a big retail segment, major responsibilities, and many cats to herd.

Then, in walks a 25-year-old kid with almost no merchandising experience, spouting some company B.S. about optimizing his business. I failed to apply Larry's lesson and show that I cared about Tony's needs. Somehow, I made the meeting all about me when I should have focused on how my project could help him achieve better results.

I had not shown him respect, yet I had expected him to respect me. But it didn't work that way in Tony's world. It was on me to prove my value. To secure his respect and cooperation, I would have to demonstrate my respect for him and prove my worth.

I focused on Tony's business area for the next few weeks, using all available data to unravel knots and explore issues. It became clear that his people, consumed by the hectic minutiae of daily tasks, were missing some important big-picture developments.

Once I had a firm grip on their problems, I asked for another meeting. May found me a 20-minute slot about two weeks out.

When the day came, I arrived armed with a binder that read like a storybook—a straightforward narrative zeroing in on the issues plaguing his business area. Graphs and spreadsheets supported my analysis. I had caught problems and developed several potential solutions. I wanted our meeting to be about the solutions, not just the problems.

I sat waiting in the same chair next to the same dusty plant. This time, I had brought plenty of work so I could be productive no matter how long the wait was. People streamed in and out of his office. I worked on other projects. The time flew by.

Finally, at 4:45 p.m., May admitted me just as Graziosi was hanging up the phone.

He glared at me. "What's this?" he snarled. "I thought, we... we already did this?"

"We did, Tony. I just need a few minutes. I'm about to send my notes on your business to the CEO, and I wanted to give you a preview in case any questions come down for you. It should only take a couple of minutes."

"Siddown."

I sat, opened the binder, turned it toward him, and pushed it across his desk.

"I know you already know most of this," I said as he scanned the page, knowing he didn't.

He held up an index finger to signal, "Give me a minute," while he studied the page. He turned to the next page and the next, reading closely, taking it in.

"This can't be right."

It was precisely the response I'd hoped for. The information was new to him, and he instantly recognized that it was meaningful.

"Let's go over there and spread out," he said, gesturing toward his conference table. He got up and started laying out pages on the table.

"May!" he yelled. "Get Claudia in here!"

A minute later, a harried-looking, older woman appeared at the door.

"Tony, what's up?"

"Did you know you have over 100 products in your department that haven't sold a single piece in the last four months?" he asked. "And another 150 that haven't sold a piece in at least half of our stores?"

"That does not seem possible. No way."

Graziosi waved some pages at her. "Check these out. Let me know if it's true."

Over the next several hours, we stayed focused on the reports while he summoned and questioned every member of his team.

It was approaching 8:00 p.m. when he looked up at me and stared silently. We were eye-to-eye for several somewhat tense moments.

Was he angry, or insulted, or what?

"Okay," he said. "You proved yourself. Sorry I gave you a hard time the other day, but everyone here is so full of shit. You and me are going to work together. A lot."

"*I don't think so!*" I was thinking. I was glad I had earned his respect, but in my mind, we were done, and my attention was already focused on another project.

But Tony Graziosi would end up becoming a strong, positive force in my professional life. And it had all started with that barrage of insults and fingernail-clipping.

Over the next year, Tony would often summon me to his office and ask my perspective on different matters. Sometimes he needed me to help him emphasize a point to a supplier or arm him with stories the data had revealed.

Maybe a year after my first encounter with Tony, my boss, Larry, called me to his office one afternoon. He was pacing when I came in.

"Okay," Larry said, "follow me."

We headed for the next office down the hall, which belonged to Eric Salus, Executive Vice President of the Home Store, Cosmetics and Fragrances. I had met Eric a few times: highly intelligent, extremely focused, a no-nonsense person who drove straight to the point. Some found him intimidating; I appreciated his directness. He would later become president of the Macy's Home Store.

As I stepped into the office, I felt an immediate tension. Tony was already sitting at the conference table near the window. His presence was intimidating. Eric sat behind an imposing desk across the room. His body language emanated authority and scrutiny. Their silence wasn't just a lack of words; it was palpable, filling the room with anticipation and unease. My nerves flared up instantly, a visceral reaction to the unknown. What could I have possibly done?

As Larry and I took seats at the table with Tony, my mind was a whirlwind of speculation. The seriousness of their demeanor hinted that I was in trouble, yet the reason was elusive and troubling. Eric glared at me from across the room as I settled into the chair. It wasn't just a look; it felt like an unspoken challenge, adding to my growing apprehension. If I knew what I had done, I would have confessed immediately.

Then came the curveball.

"Evan, Tony wants you as his DMM for Housewares," Eric said. "But I don't think you have enough experience--"

Tony groaned. "Don't screw yourself, Eric!"

DMMs, or Divisional Merchandise Managers run a large product area and manage four to six buyers. Jeff Moore was my DMM at Lord & Taylor. Typically, DMMs have vast experience and a long track record in the buying office. The odds of me landing a DMM position had seemed slim. To have a shot, I figured I would have to take a step back and prove myself as a buyer all over again, possibly for several years. That prospect was unappealing, so I kept my focus on the job at hand.

"I think Tony knows what Evan can do," Larry said.

"This is the guy you want for the job!" Tony barked. "Trust me, Eric! I have 100 percent confidence in this guy."

I had not seen it coming, but I certainly believed I could handle the job, and it was gratifying to hear Tony and Larry arguing my case. Their confidence made me want the position badly, but Eric seemed dubious. Eventually, he said he would "think about it," which I took as a bad sign since Eric was usually so decisive.

To my surprise, I was promoted to vice president, divisional merchandise manager of Housewares the very next day—a turning point in my career. It started me down the path to becoming a player in the industry where years later, I would launch my own business. I could not have been more elated.

I settled into a vacant office next to Tony's in the non-glamour wing and made it my business to learn as much as possible from one of the best execs in the industry.

I'd hardly settled in before heading to Los Angeles for the Gourmet Show, a culinary trade show. I was flying from JFK, Tony from Newark, and we planned to meet on the first night for a dinner hosted by All-Clad, a premier cookware manufacturer. The dinner was to celebrate the launch of their latest cookware line—a collection developed with the Celebrity Chef and Food Network star Emeril Lagasse.

It was my first time in L.A., and I was thrilled to be there. Sometimes, L.A. can seem to be the most beautiful city in the world, and when I arrived, the air was clear, and the light was amazing. I checked into my hotel and grabbed a cab to Hollywood for the evening's festivities.

At the destination, I was guided to an elevator that opened to a stunning rooftop venue, more appropriate for a celebrity wedding than a business dinner. I stood gawking as the setting sun cast a warm glow on the Hollywood Hills. I heard someone call my name and turned to see Tony by the bar, gesturing me over.

"Welcome to L.A.!" he said, giving me a hug.

Drinks in hand, we stood looking out over the Hills. I thanked him for the opportunity to work for him.

"With me! You work *with* me, Evan. Not *for* me," he corrected.

He told me the DMM position had remained vacant for over a year. "I needed the right person. Someone with guts and passion. Someone with integrity. Look, Evan, we are partners now. I know everyone in this business, and I'm gonna make sure they know you. We are going to be a force to be reckoned with."

Tony's style was to treat his people like family, demanding dedication and loyalty in return. It seemed a fair exchange, and that evening, he introduced me to the who's-who of our industry in the most gracious manner.

"Meet my new business partner, Evan Dash, the brightest VP I've ever worked with. The future of the company. When this guy speaks, he speaks for both of us."

It was an unforgettable night. I spent time with Emeril and his soon-to-be wife, Alden—two of the most genuine and grounded individuals I had ever met. Later, in the wee hours at the hotel bar, I watched Tony chop it up with DMX and the Rough Riders as if they were long-lost kin. I was on cloud nine.

Those three days in L.A. were a whirlwind, and I fell in love with the Housewares industry. It packed more excitement than any other category I had experienced, and it was an incredible era for the industry. The Food Network had just launched its round-the-clock channel, connecting millions of viewers to the delights of food and cooking. They were elevating chefs to celebrity status and inspiring people to embrace time in the kitchen as a pastime instead of a chore.

On the return flight to New York, I thought about how it had started with Tony. The guy who kicked me out of his office had become my strongest advocate. Tony was genuinely interested in my future. He had my back, and the lesson was clear—you must show respect before you earn respect. And earning respect puts you on the road to success.

Takeaways

RESPECT RESPECT

- **See all sides.**
  From my initial point of view, my Tony problem was all his fault. Socks on the desk? Nail clippers? Really? But when I considered the situation from Tony's side of the desk, I saw that showing up with nothing to offer except my own self-importance was a waste of his time. And for an experienced senior executive who took his job seriously, it was an insult. Once I saw my Tony problem from his point of view, I realized I was to blame. For my next encounter with Tony, I showed up with a new approach and vital intel he could use. Tony saw my value and changed his attitude, allowing us to become friends and allies instead of adversaries.

- **Embrace conflict to earn respect.**
  Conflict can be destructive and a waste of time. But when properly managed, it can also be a catalyst for growth, understanding, and relationship-building. Honest conflict helps teams generate ferocious new ideas.

I mistakenly believed my fancy title would guarantee Tony's respect, so I cruised into his office, flaunted my self-importance, presented my agenda, and offered him nothing. He was a busy executive, and I had wasted his time, so he threw us into conflict, forcing me to retreat. I made the second appointment, determined to earn Tony's respect. I demonstrated that I wasn't intimidated, but also showed I heard him loud and clear by generating useful information. No one had ever handled Tony quite that way, and soon, I had earned his respect and, eventually, his trust and mentorship.

- **Embrace people whose strengths match your weaknesses.**
  Tony's self-awareness was admirable. He sought a business partner who could complement his expertise and support him in the areas where he wasn't as knowledgeable. Despite his tough-guy demeanor, Tony thirsted for knowledge and had no problem learning from someone half his age. He valued my strengths and figured they more than made up for my lack of experience. And, as he predicted in L.A., we did become a force to be reckoned with.

8. Win-Wins

In 1902, the De'Longhi family established their namesake kitchenware brand in Treviso, Italy. When I assumed my new role as Divisional Merchandise Manager at Macy's, their century-old brand generated over $1 billion in annual revenue globally and was positioned as an icon of the Housewares industry.

One of my first meetings was with Jim McCusker, the President of De'Longhi America. As an American from outside the family, Jim was a rare bird in the top ranks at De'Longhi. A veteran of the company and our industry, he was nearly a quarter of a century into his tenure.

Jim shared their brand's story and the relationship our companies once enjoyed. Macy's had been De'Longhi's premier American retailer, but over the last decade, the business had waned as misunderstandings and squabbles took center stage.

I listened to Jim's concerns and ideas. Together, we conceived a plan to breathe new life into their brand at Macy's. The centerpiece would be a new De'Longhi shop in

Macy's Herald Square flagship. With the opportunity ahead, both sides' frustration turned to excitement as we prepared for a re-launch the following year, our respective teams devoting themselves to the vision.

Six months after that re-launch, the De'Longhi family traveled to the United States to tour their Herald Square shop. I wanted them to know how much we valued the relationship, so I orchestrated a red-carpet reception in the opulent boardroom of the Chairman's wing and introduced the family to Macy's senior management.

Down on the sales floor, the De'Longhis were amazed by the space I had allotted to their brand and thrilled by what Jim had done with it. The family assured us it was one of their finest displays worldwide.

My job was easy. I had only offered Jim the prime retail real estate. He and his people took it over, producing results that made us both look great. Together, we created something for both companies to be proud of.

Within a year of starting in Housewares, I had hit my stride. When Tony Graziosi left Macy's for a top position at JC Penney, Eric didn't award anyone Tony's job. Instead, he had me report directly to him, which felt like a strong vote of confidence. Eric and I built a great working rapport. He was smart and tough, with a BS detector that was always on. Eric cut through the crap, although his method could be a little rough—less surgeon, more artisanal butcher.

Eric taught me things that Tony Graziosi didn't or couldn't. Tony was all about building and maintaining strategic relationships. Eric taught me to read the fine print and know the details. *"Retail is detail"* was one of the mantras. Whenever I met with him, I had to back up every claim I made with facts that were often hidden in the data, waiting to be unearthed and given attention.

My basic strategy at Macy's was to allow our suppliers to do exactly what they claimed to be best at—then hold them accountable for sales. The De'Longhis were all about creating exceptional kitchenware and selling it with in-store displays that pulsed with their unique style. I had been able to offer Jim the space he needed to sell a lot more, and he had produced a big win for both of us.

The strategy was working, but after a couple of years, I started to get antsy. I was fighting an uphill battle in the world of department store retailing. Big box retailers had become all the rage for Housewares. With their off-mall locations, shopping carts, and everyday low prices, chains like Bed Bath and Beyond offered a more effortless shopping experience, and consumers could not ignore the allure. My faith in the future of the department store was starting to wane.

My numbers were strong, but the overall business at Macy's wasn't flourishing. At a weekly staff meeting, Eric told his seven DMMs that no bonuses would be paid that year. I lingered behind after the meeting to plead my case as an exception.

As a relatively new DMM, I still earned a "league minimum" salary despite producing excellent results.

As expected, Eric was unmoved.

And the moment I stepped back into my office, my telephone began ringing. It was before the days of caller ID, but I took my chances and answered.

"Evan Dash."

"Hello Evan, this is Heidi from Linens 'n Things. You've been on our radar, and our Chief of Merchandising would love to meet with you. Any chance you could meet her for breakfast in the city tomorrow morning?"

"Yes. I can make that happen. The Red Flame Diner at 7:30 a.m.?"

"Perfect. Audrey will be there."

I probably wouldn't have agreed to meet Audrey if I hadn't just come out of the disappointing meeting with Eric. And that evening, a sense of regret began to gnaw at me. I wanted to cancel but hadn't gotten Heidi's phone number.

And the following day, Audrey Schlaepfer and I had an intriguing conversation over breakfast. She had recently joined Linens 'n Things from Warner Brothers. She had massive enthusiasm for the big box model. Her ideas sounded remarkable, and her excitement was contagious.

Over the next two weeks, I navigated a rigorous interview process for the position of General Merchandise Manager—the same job Eric had at Macy's. Whoever got the job at Linens 'n Things would be responsible for half of their business.

Despite the phone call and the breakfast, I didn't expect serious consideration. I was only 28, and there were many more experienced and accomplished merchants in our industry.

I had meetings with ten people, including a store walk-through with their President, Steven Silverstein, one of the sharpest minds I have ever encountered, who challenged almost every opinion and idea I expressed while sharing his own insights into the business. Even if I wasn't going to get the job, I figured the experience had been well worth my time.

Several weeks later, I learned that the company was divided on whether to hire me. Some—including Steven—were uneasy about my limited experience. So, they gave themselves another weekend to reflect and would decide on Monday.

Over that weekend, Steven visited one of their stores, bumping into one of their prominent suppliers, who just happened to be my friend Jim McCusker, President of De'longhi. After a little small talk, Steven confided that they were considering me for a GMM position.

Without hesitation, Jim told Steven to hire me. Jim said I had the planning and strategy skills to perfectly complement my product and marketing instincts. He told Steven how I had helped him transform his business and delivered on everything I'd promised—a rare quality in retailing.

It was perfect timing.

On Monday, I received a call from Heidi asking me to come in for one more meeting with their CEO, Norman Axelrod. We had a great conversation, and they made me an offer on the spot. I had spent twenty-plus hours being interviewed and thought my performance in those meetings had swayed them. But it was Steven's five-minute encounter with Jim in a Linens 'n Things big box on Long Island that had clinched the job for me.

Takeaways

WIN-WINS

- **Rely on people vested in your success.**
  While I had the opportunity to significantly influence the De'Longhi shop within Macy's—its design, inventory, and operations—I recognized the value of expertise. Instead of relying on my limited experience in Housewares, I turned it over to someone with over 30 years of expertise with his brand. Jim was in tune with De'Longhi's success nationwide and had a pulse on the optimal approach for Macy's. Building a world-class shop in our Herald Square Flagship would be a major feather in his cap with the De'Longhi family, and I knew it was important to him. By collaborating with a skilled vendor who had skin in the game, I could direct my attention to other ventures, confident Jim would deliver exactly what we both needed.

- **Your reputation is a personal PR department.**
  Who are you? Word travels fast, and what other people say about you always carries more weight than anything you can say about yourself. "It takes 20 years to build a reputation," Warren Buffet said, "and five minutes to ruin it." People you do business with will remember when you help them. And they'll never forget if you hurt them. Your reputation can create opportunities—and shut

them down even faster. Once I got the backstory of Steven and Jim's chance meeting, I realized it wasn't me who earned the job offer—it was my reputation.

- **You're entitled to your own opinion, but the facts are the facts.**
  When Eric grilled me on the details, I quickly realized that a lot of what people say and semi-believe has zero grounding in the facts. People aren't being deliberately deceitful, just susceptible to preconceived notions, gut feelings, and lazy thinking. Making good decisions takes facts—not assumptions. Facts are where you find solutions. The data always has plenty to say, and I love working with people who are willing to listen to it.

9. Burning Down the House

When I left Macy's for Linens 'n Things, the "I quit" conversation with Eric was tense. He didn't want to accept the change and was understandably upset. He had given me the opportunity that led me to an even better opportunity.

After trying and failing to persuade me to stay, Eric said some harsh things in the heat of the moment. My firefighter training gave me the calm and clarity I needed during a stressful encounter, and I remained calm, which prevented an escalation. Firefighters put out fires; we don't feed them.

A department store aims to seduce people the moment they push through the revolving doors, immediately bombarding shoppers with tantalizing sights, sounds, and scents. But the labyrinthian pathways of the sales floor and the sheer abundance of everything can be overwhelming. Department stores can be exciting, but they're not for everyone.

Mass retailers like Target and Walmart are more straightforward—one huge floor plan organized into aisles brimming with selections. Wide aisles make it easy for shoppers to find what they came for and get out fast, with the average consumer visiting only a few of the aisles.

But the racetrack design of the American big box store seemed like retail perfection to me. The genius of the racetrack design was its fluidity and ease of navigation—no need to crisscross a maze of aisles or hunt high and low on a sprawling sales floor. Everything in the big box was laid out to gently guide people through the entire store, one section to the next. This efficient, intuitive model boosted the shopper's experience, encouraging exploration and discovery of exciting new products.

At Linens 'n Things, we were all about the racetrack. Our floor plan led the customer through the entire store from entrance to register. It gave us plenty of opportunities to surprise and delight our shoppers. We also provided shopping carts like a supermarket, expecting people to buy more than they could carry.

Linens 'n Things circa 2001 was a merchant's dream. To say I loved my job would be an understatement. In just two years, I doubled my business while learning the ins and outs of product development and manufacturing. The future looked exciting, and I planned to stick around.

The last thing I expected was the phone call I received from Eric, my old boss at Macy's.

"You ready to come back yet?"

What? I rocked back in my chair and checked that my office door was closed. I held the receiver a little closer and may have even whispered.

"Are you serious? I thought I burned my bridges."

"Oh, come on, Evan, you're not still sulking—"

"*I'm* sulking? You told me I'd never work for you or Macy's again."

Eric had been upset when I resigned from Macy's. And when Eric was upset, he tended to use colorful language. Our last encounter had been memorable.

And now, out of the blue, he was on my office phone, and I was perplexed. I knew he had to be aware of my success at Linens 'n Things. My old job as a DMM would have been a step backward. I knew Eric was too smart to waste any time on that.

And I was right.

"Macy's is embarking on the boldest initiative in the industry. We're going to centralize our buying into one world-class organization in New York. I've just been named president."

"Wow, congrats Eric! I'm thrilled for–"

"Shut up, Evan," he said calmly. "You still talk too much. You want to be thrilled? How about senior vice president and general merchandise manager?"

Boom! I was speechless. With one sentence, Eric had changed the entire equation and maybe my life.

"Evan, you are going to restore *The Cellar* to its rightful place as the absolute top-tier destination of the nation for housewares."

My favorite business category. My sweet spot. And Eric knew it.

Back in the Seventies, *The Cellar* had transformed Macy's into a home products destination by introducing a gourmet kitchenware space into the once-humdrum kitchen utensil aisles. Launched in the San Francisco flagship store, *The Cellar* took its cues from iconic European department stores like Harrods and Le Bon Marché. The Cellar was quickly installed in Macy's stores nationwide—stocked with beautiful cookware, small kitchen appliances, and tableware. In *The Cellar,* there was always a treat for the senses waiting around every corner, with countless impulse items complementing the big-ticket appliances.

"*The Cellar* was and still is a great concept," Eric said. "Execution has been lousy. We must bring it back to what it was, then take it to another level. Your DMMs and buyers will do the centralized purchasing for all the stores —no more region-by-region buying. You and I hand-pick the best of the buying staff. You lead one supercharged team, stocking all the different product areas for every *Cellar* in the country. Sound like a plan?"

Yes, it did.

We met for dinner a few nights later. Eric was one of the rare executives who grasped the details of a business in fine grain and still led with vision. His plan was undoubtedly the most exciting shake-up of our industry since I'd joined the retail world.

A few days later, I accepted a formal job offer, even though I still couldn't quite believe it was actually happening—a Senior VP at Macy's with a mission to reinvent an iconic business? It was surreal until I received the FedEx box with my welcome packet, including an employment contract. That brought me back to earth.

It was the longest, thickest legal document I had ever held. In previous jobs, I never signed anything beyond a small employment agreement—one or two pages. These inevitably came with an employee handbook I always planned to read but never did.

But this thing was a dense hunk of paperwork drafted in high legalese, with pages listing restrictive covenants packed with terms like *non-disclosure, non-disparagement, non-competition,* and *non-solicitation.*

A whole lot of *nons*. And they all seemed designed to prohibit me from pursuing future opportunities where my expertise would be valuable.

That started me worrying. What if things at Macy's didn't go as planned? I was sure it would, but what if it didn't? How would I find another job if they locked me into such a restrictive contract?

I felt squeezed. Trapped. Claustrophobic. Short of breath. So I called Eric.

"Hey, I just got your indentured servitude contract."

"Don't worry about it, Evan. It's standard boilerplate at the senior executive levels," he said calmly. "Everyone signs it."

"I'm not comfortable with it. Look, you want me at Macy's, and I'm thrilled. I want to be at Macy's. But what if it doesn't work out?"

"Evan, when you reach a certain level, the company has a right to insist on another level of commitment. Think about it. You represent a huge investment for us. And we're offering a severance payment for the entire term of your contract if things don't go as planned."

"But I don't want a severance package. I want to be able to go out and find a new job if things don't work out. I can't afford to lose my career momentum."

Momentum isn't just something; it's everything. Momentum is hard to build. It takes time, intention, and determination. And once you have momentum, things always seem to roll your way. The world throws opportunities at you.

I knew losing momentum in my career would be a disaster. Eric and I went back and forth on that damn contract for several weeks until he finally gave up.

"If you don't want to sign it, don't sign it," he said, throwing his hands up.

So, I put it out of sight and focused on my job. Which did not turn out to be what I had hoped for.

Implementing a new vision in a legacy business would never go according to plan. We were trying to act like a start-up while operating within five different operating companies. Almost overnight, we became responsible for Macy's East, Macy's West, Rich's/Lazarus/Goldsmith's in Atlanta, Burdine's in Florida, and The Bon Marche in the Pacific Northwest, all operating as separate companies, each with unique challenges. We inherited five different systems producing information in five different formats. It was impossible to analyze data across the entire chain efficiently.

We had expected dealing with suppliers would be much easier, but that wasn't the case. Five different buyers had made five different commitments to their suppliers, and no one appreciated our new team trying to renegotiate existing deals. The process was going to produce uncertainty and cause casualties. There were going to be major winners; there were going to be major losers.

We also faced powerful headwinds from inside the company. Our initiative had people worried that many regional and specialized jobs would be eliminated in favor of a leaner, centralized team. And they were right: If our experiment worked, jobs would be at risk. So loyal employees with long tenure suddenly had reason to second-guess their job security, which didn't exactly create the atmosphere we needed for success.

The headwinds put Eric under tremendous pressure, and the tough days and weeks took a toll on him. The company had built him a presidential suite roughly the size of my house. It had everything, so he rarely left his side of the floor. That's why I was surprised when Eric suddenly appeared at my office door one afternoon.

"How the hell did you find your way down here from your palace, Eric?"

"I asked where to find that cocky kid who thinks he fucking knows everything." He stepped into my office, shut the door, took a folder from under his arm, and placed it on my desk.

It was the contract I had refused to sign the year before.

"Sign the fucking paper, Evan."

I saw the look in his eyes and suddenly knew Eric's days at the company were numbered, and he was protecting me. If he left, my days could be numbered too. And the severance package was, after all, a kind of parachute. It was better than just being tossed out of the plane.

So, I signed the three copies, which already had his signature. He left one with me, put the other two back in the folder, and left as quickly as he'd entered.

The fact that he had remembered that I was without a contract and circled back to make me sign the damn thing was a protective and selfless act. It spoke volumes about his character—especially when he was on his way out and owed me nothing.

I was lucky to have a boss like Eric. He had given me opportunity after opportunity and rewarded my performance and loyalty with promotions, raises, and bonuses. He had a more significant impact on my professional growth and financial well-being than anyone else. But what I was most thankful for was that he had my back. Throughout my entire work experience, there was no better feeling than knowing that my boss had my back.

It was strange, but I felt tremendous relief as soon as I signed the contract. Eric clearly had doubts about his future and his ability to protect me. With the contract signed, I had something to land on. Without it, I would have been at risk.

Six months later, Eric left Macy's. His replacement was another senior executive from within the company. Even though I was "Eric's guy," I was confident of my future. During our first one-on-one meeting, my new boss asked how things were going, and I decided to offer him the real goods, focusing heavily on the negative. I imagined it would be helpful for him to know the problems I was dealing with, but my answer pegged me as a complainer —a problems guy, not a solutions guy. It made a poor first impression and set the tone for a relationship that only worsened.

I could have hit the reset button. It would have been easy to schedule an appointment and apologize for that first dispiriting interaction. I could have started a dialogue focused on problem-solving instead of problems. I could have asked for his support and helped him understand our challenges—without complaining.

I could have done many things to improve the relationship, but I was too proud to try them. I held a massive sense of superiority based on my strong numbers. I refused to fit into the subordinate role he wanted me to play because I figured I knew more about the business than he did. Our exchanges were increasingly awkward and uncomfortable; it was no surprise, given my attitude.

Once a week, I delivered a progress update that neglected to report on the tasks he had assigned. I felt I had more important things to do. As he became more frustrated with me, I became more arrogant with him. I was a top performer in the company, right? I felt entitled.

Eventually, things started to settle down. The tough early work my team had done was beginning to pay off. We had established an excellent working tempo with all the regional operating companies, and my new boss was making a positive difference that people around the organization could feel. Even I had to admit that he was doing well. I began to think I might stick around for the long haul.

Then came a giant announcement. Macy's had acquired the second largest department store conglomerate in America, the May Department Stores Company. When I started at Lord & Taylor, it was a division of The May Company, so, ironically, my career had now come full circle.

The news was exciting, but it meant a return to the tedious and intricate process of integrating a new business. I could see the challenges coming at us. We'd be operating across multiple systems again, assembling and scrutinizing a vast array of new data while holding the hands of anxious suppliers. It was déjà vu, but I was up for the challenge.

The following months *were* exciting, with a steep learning curve. I spent weeks working with my team on a strategy to merge the strengths of both companies and grow the combined entity to new heights. I was doing some of the best and most challenging work of my career. Department store retailing was tough, but my plan was energizing. However, when I presented it to my boss, it felt like I ran into a wall.

"You completely ignored the direction I wanted you to follow," he said in a pained voice, almost a whisper.

"I evaluated it, but my plan will capture much more business. Your direction could leave hundreds of millions of dollars on the table."

"Then we'll have to plan it that way and let the business seek the right level for how I want it run," he said matter of factly.

Plan it *down?* Come on. I saw our business growing. Massively. It was there for the taking, so I tried to illustrate my points with examples, but he shut me down each time.

Finally, discouraged, deflated, and too frustrated to argue, I left the office and walked along 34th Street to Penn Station to catch my train back to the 'burbs. I had never felt so defeated; it felt like my world was crashing down. I had been working 16-hour days but falling further behind on everything I needed to do. I had two little boys at home who were my world, but I hardly saw them during the week. My wife and I grew further apart, and our marriage was crumbling. Work was no longer fun; it was drudgery. I couldn't fathom planning my business *down* when I could see a road to growth ahead of us. It felt like accepting a loss when victory was within reach.

I faced a dilemma. If I quit, all the restrictions in my contract would trigger. I wouldn't be able to land a great new job in my field. And I didn't want to make a career change.

There was only one way out. I had to get him to fire me. If he fired me, I would have a long period of severance to figure out my life. It would be my best chance to pursue an entrepreneurial future without the typical risk. Bills would get paid, and I'd have the time to make moves. Until then, I had to go in every day and give it my all. I focused on trying to deliver the best results for the company but did it my way, mostly ignoring his instructions. It made every interaction unpleasant for both of us. I didn't care. I saw myself as a superstar gone rogue, ignoring my timid coach and focusing only on delivering a win.

Finally, one Friday afternoon, I got the message I'd been expecting for months in the form of a little yellow sticky note on my desk. *See him at 5:30 today,* written in red.

I walked in, knowing what was coming, but I still couldn't believe it. After hearing the words, "You're fired," I felt an immediate lightness. All of my stress melted away. I felt reborn. But this would be short-lived.

There was no blow-up. Security wasn't waiting to escort me out of the building. My now ex-boss was a gracious gentleman and treated me with dignity, suggesting I take a week to wrap things up. Instead, I worked the next three to ensure my team would be okay. Then, on my last day, as usual among the last to leave, I switched off the lights, walked out the door, and into my future.

Takeaways

BURNING DOWN THE HOUSE

- **Don't burn your bridges.**
  Regardless of which side you find yourself on, your mission is to stay cool and de-escalate tense situations. When I left Macy's for Linens 'n Things, Eric took it badly. Things got heated. But a nasty argument takes two, and I stayed calm. And that meant that when Eric needed someone with my skills for a bigger job, he could easily bring me back to Macy's. If we had torched our relationship, I would never have received the call to come back.

- **I got your back.**
  My friend and leadership coach, Dr. Gary McGrath, asserts the importance of an "I got your back" culture in his book, *Leading from the Front*. Both of our backgrounds—his in the military and mine in emergency services—rely on this principle. When lives—not just bonuses—are on the line, an "I got your back" culture is non-negotiable. But in the corporate workplace, such unwavering trust is rare. When Eric forced me to sign the contract, it came out of left field and demonstrated that he did have my back 100 percent. Working with people who have your back builds trust and confidence. It inspires loyalty from a team who feel supported and creates an environment where people can do their best work.

- **First impressions matter.**
  Given the opportunity to make a great first impression on my new boss at Macy's, I made a giant miscalculation. Instead of demonstrating initiative, I sought sympathy. I should have looked back to my first meeting with Tony Graziosi and focused on what I could do for my new boss, not what I needed from him. Instead of complaining, I should have demonstrated that I was capable, loyal, insightful, and ready to champion our success together. But nothing I did or said led him to that conclusion, and his mind was made up about me right then and there—I was one of the problems he would have to deal with.

10. Clarity

I left Macy's on a sugar high, with a severance package and newfound freedom, but without realizing how traumatic and devastating being fired actually was. The next morning, it hit. No job. No office. Nowhere to go.

In the days and weeks following, I felt like someone riding a train through a long, dark tunnel. The light at the end of the tunnel was a speck. Sometimes it wasn't there at all. It was like passing through the stages of grief.

First, shock and denial. I spent my first jobless days pacing around the house, trying to wrap my head around what had just happened. After a few days, boredom set in, and numbness and shock gave way to anger. I'd been running the top-performing business in the whole company; how could they fire *me*? I neglected to see that I gave them little choice.

I kept replaying the last conversation with my boss, thinking of all the clever and brutal things I could have said. The more I fantasized about striking back, the more powerless I felt, which stirred up more anger. I was caught in a nasty loop, but gradually, the anger gave way to the genuine emotion underneath—sadness. I was grieving. I had lost my job, and with it, my identity. I felt rejected and abandoned. My self-confidence had taken a massive hit. I felt paralyzed professionally. I had no place to go in the morning. No agenda stacked with meetings, no important calls to make. Zero deadlines to meet. No data to interrogate. No fabulous outcomes to pursue. I felt alone and empty, which brought me back to those dreary days I had spent exiled in the hall outside my elementary school classroom. I could almost smell the must of industrial cleaner, school lunches, and floor wax—the scent of expulsion and failure.

Three weeks later, Thanksgiving arrived, and I felt even more detached. I wasn't exactly in the mood. For years, so much of my time had revolved around developing strategies for Black Friday, the official holiday season kickoff. Retailers put tremendous effort into this one shopping day when, historically, the red ink would miraculously turn black, transforming 46 weeks of losses into profits. Macy's had created Black Friday, and Macy's was the home of Thanksgiving.

Macy's held their first Thanksgiving parade in 1924 with animals from the Central Park Zoo. The elephants and zebras were eventually replaced by the balloons that still float to Herald Square every Thanksgiving morning while America prepares for its turkey feast.

The strategy was to kick off the holiday season by inviting shoppers into Macy's on the Friday after Thanksgiving when the doors reopened at dawn. It was wildly successful, and the Parade and Black Friday remain important American rituals to this day.

I knew I was going to visit Macy's on Black Friday. I was still a retail guy—I needed to know what was happening in the stores and gauge the pulse of the market. It was in my blood. I couldn't stay away.

I woke up early. I wanted to get to the stores by 6:00 a.m. I brought a brand-new notebook, symbolic of the new career I hadn't yet figured out how to launch.

I arrived at Macy's in the Roosevelt Field Mall in Garden City, New York, around 5:30 a.m. The lines already stretched down the sidewalk as people geared up to make their sprint to scoop up as many killer deals as possible. That year was all about the "Door-Buster," a new term for products offered at impossibly low prices and only available "while supplies last."

Out there in the parking lot, the sheer lunacy—not to mention cynicism—of what Black Friday had become struck me hard. In that era of flailing retail stores, most, not just Macy's, had adopted mail-in rebates as a marketing strategy. The consumer could only get the lowest advertised price *if* they mailed in a rebate form and then waited six to eight weeks to get a check to refund the difference between the advertised price and what they actually paid.

These promotions were terrific for the retailer because few shoppers noticed the fine print about the rebates, and only a small fraction would ever take the time to mail in for their refund. So, people were lining up innocently to take advantage of the savings that they would have to jump through several hoops to get. The stores counted on human nature and holiday distractions to gain an unfair and undeserved advantage.

Sooner or later, many customers would realize they had been treated with something less than respect.

While I sat in my car, watching people jogging in place and hugging their kids to keep them warm, the realization sank in—by fighting so hard to help the store win the battle of Black Friday, I had been losing the battle for customer loyalty—the only fight that should have counted.

In years past, I would have walked through the employee entrance, showed my ID, and had full run of the store. It had always been such a thrilling moment, waiting inside the store for the doors to open to the rush and excitement my team had worked so hard to create.

But this Black Friday had me feeling disenchanted and even a little ripped-off like many of my customers must have felt when they got to the register. Professionally, I had hit rock bottom. At the same time, I realized that many people who had brought their children to the retail equivalent of the Running of the Bulls probably had no choice but to line up for these deceptively low prices. Maybe it was the only way they could afford presents for everyone on their list. No doubt some were single parents —moms and dads just trying to do right by their kids.

At that moment, I realized I had never tried to humanize our customers while building our marketing campaigns. I'd been obsessed with beating the competition and hitting my sales targets. I had been playing to win but on the wrong playing field. Maybe I ought to have been advocating for my customers and delivering *more* than they expected, not less. Certainly not leaving them with a feeling they'd been conned.

When the doors finally opened that morning, and all the shoppers had piled through, I went inside to look around. I stood near the cash registers to watch what people were buying, and I wanted to be close enough to overhear what they were saying. And boy, did I get an earful.

Five out of the first six customers in line complained that they were charged more than the advertised price. They felt deceived and taken advantage of—and they were right.

At Lord & Taylor, I had disapproved of coupons because I knew they were damaging the brand. But at Macy's, I had gone all in on a strategy that was creating parking lots full of dissatisfied customers from coast to coast. It didn't matter that every retailer was doing the very same thing. Our customers were mad at Macy's, and it was a feeling they would not soon forget.

And mail-in rebates weren't just a pain for customers. The situation put the sales staff in a terrible position. On an ordinary day, those were challenging jobs. With a mail-in rebate promotion running on Black Friday, our hard-working frontline employees had to absorb all the venom spewed by angry customers.

At the same time, the executives in the buying office only saw the numbers on their computer screens, missing the real and damaging consequences playing out on selling floors across the country.

How could we put our customers and employees in that position and still expect their loyalty? We had committed the two cardinal sins of retail. We broke the faith of our customers by undermining their trust. And we had created a hostile work environment for our employees. I was so focused on beating my numbers that I failed to see what a terrible strategy I put in place.

I wandered into the mall in a daze, grabbed a coffee, and retreated to my car. My heart and mind were racing. Something major was shifting in how I understood my career and my purpose. I cracked open my brand-new notebook and started scribbling the foundation of a brand-new approach for an industry.

BLACK FRIDAY

My strategy—all wrong. Huge mistake. Tunnel vision. My approach took the joy away from countless families to start their holiday season. Blinded by numbers. Obsessed with competition. I undermined my company and my responsibility as a leader.

Customers have endless choices. Respect them. Win their hearts. Earn their loyalty. Treasure it. Don't take it for granted—EVER!

Sitting behind the steering wheel, excitement filled me from within. All the negativity I had been carrying like a weight suddenly washed away in a wave of clarity that felt like a superpower. For years, I imagined a future as a business owner. Well, the future was now, and I was scribbling down the code for what would become the secret to my success as an entrepreneur.

Don't aim for wallets; aim to win hearts!

That bitterly cold November morning was the most pivotal moment of my professional life. In the solitude of the Macy's parking lot, I accepted the realization that it was time to carve my own path. As I continued to write, I made three vows that would become the core of the style of servant leadership I aspired to embody:

I would practice self-awareness and compassion.

I would create an environment where team members would be inspired, respected, and empowered to do great work.

I would never lose sight of our customers' needs while working tirelessly to exceed their expectations.

For the next several weeks, I worked around the clock, brainstorming business ideas and analyzing all the marketplace data I could get my hands on. My energy rivaled that of my childhood self, only now I was able to channel it into creativity and progress. The more I worked and the more I thought, the more confident I became that I could carve a niche in which to make my mark.

With my confidence peaked, I finally mustered up the courage I needed to get started for real. I walked into my local Chase branch, opened a business account, and bet my life savings on my new philosophy of winning hearts. My company would turn fresh ideas into great products bound for stores near and far. I named the company StoreBound and registered it as an LLC.

I had gone from running a multi-billion-dollar corporate business with thousands of employees to being the self-appointed CEO of a venture that existed only on paper. Before getting anywhere near the first dollar of revenue, I would need to sort out office space, hiring, product development, manufacturing, contracts, finance, marketing, social media, and global logistics, and delve into many other areas in which I lacked expertise. No generous employment contract to sign or not sign. No severance package this time around. If I crashed and burned, I'd lose not only my job but pretty much everything I had worked years for.

I could not wait to get started.

Takeaways

CLARITY

- **Deal with the reel.**
I didn't expect to be reeling, but weeks after being fired, I still was. I was also seething with anger. In retrospect, every moment indulging myself with semi-righteous anger was time wasted. And all the time spent recounting the depressing series of events that led to my getting the chop was time wasted. All the "what if" moments were—that's right—time wasted.

    Going back into stores and connecting with the world of retail allowed me to clear my head and start thinking strategically about the future. A setback can lead you to a dead end. It can also stoke the energy you need to leap forward. Every successful person I know has suffered at least one significant setback. What made them successful was what they did next.

- **Envision and embrace the future.**
Once you have it in your sight, never lose focus. I saw my future that morning in the parking lot. Neglecting customers' needs had become the norm for big retail, allowing me to create a business based on very different values. Treating the customer with compassion and respect would be my differentiator and the cornerstone of my offering.

My early days as a fireman in 1991.

Fire Chief William Csaszar commanding the scene while other firefighters and I work to extinguish the blaze.

In 1945, at Lord & Taylor, Dorothy Shaver became the first woman to take the helm of a major retailer.

Lord & Taylor Fifth Avenue Flagship when I started my career.

Once an American retail mainstay, by 2018, Lord & Taylor had declared bankrupcy.

Holiday shoppers line up outside Macy's in 1939. An American retail legend, Macy's was *the* destination for holiday shopping.

Leading a great team at Macy's as their SVP at age 30.

November 11, 2010—
the first day of StoreBound.
Our generously sized
closet/office is where
we started the company.

With Cat Reinhard and Caitlin Wise of the Dash Marketing Team on an early video shoot in 2013. My parents volunteered their home as our set.

Our first trade show in 2012. We had our designers at desks rendering products during the show.

ON THE SET
Rachel and I debuting an early model of our egg cooker on the Home Shopping Network in 2014.

Rachel and I shooting a promotional video for investors in 2018.

Rachel and I visiting factories in 2023.

Geoffrey Zakarian photographed at StoreBound studios for the Zakarian by Dash Cookware Collection.

The launch of StoreBound's partnership with Iron Chef Geoffrey Zakarian on QVC— live from the Housewares Show.

Geoffrey Zakarian sells out another product on "In the Kitchen with David Venable" on QVC.

With Rachel, Geoffrey Zakarian and David Venable at the International Home & Housewares show.

Partnerships can be magical when you have fun together.

The Dash team on Governors Island for a volunteer event with Billion Oyster Project.

The team hard at work sorting oyster shells that will be used to repopulate NY Harbor and clean the Hudson River.

GIVING BACK TO THE COMMUNITY
The Dash team in action at City Harvest on Better World Day.

Before the International Home & Housewares Show, lots of work to be done.

Our booth showcased the Dash Brand as we envisioned it in a retail store.

STOREBOUND LEADERS
Glenn De Stefano, Rachel Dash, Evan Dash and Cat Reinhard.

Evan Dash presents to potential investors at the Nasdaq.

Dash leaders at the Nasdaq.

Venus WIlliams takes the stage to present her brand, Eleven.

Venus Williams, Billy Busko, and others at the Dash presentation.

The Dash leaders and Billy Busko enjoy dinner in France the evening before their presentation to Groupe SEB.

Geoffrey and Margaret Zakarian working with Rachel Dash in the Groupe SEB food lab.

Dash team working in the technology center of a Groupe SEB factory.

Groupe SEB World Headquarters in Écully, France.

Groupe SEB Chairman Thierry de La Tour d'Artaise

Groupe SEB CEO Stanislas de Gramont

The office space we took over in 2020 was in shambles, but we knew it had amazing potential.

Our goal was to create an inspiring workspace that reflected our brand identity.

We asked our designers to create their ideal work environment.

The end result showcased our company values and supported our culture of collaboration and creativity.

A big THANK YOU to our amazing team and all of our retailers and customers for the years of support.
—Evan & Rachel Dash

11. Perfectly Paired

One of my favorite business reads is Simon Sinek's "Start with Why." Sinek writes that for a company to achieve customer loyalty and long-term success, the business needs a "Visionary" and an "Operator," two identities originally defined by Les McKeown in his book, "Predictable Success."

The Visionary is the front-facing, charismatic, big-idea person—the dreamer, the brainstormer, the risk taker, and, most likely, the founder. While such folks can be over-simplifiers, they also supply the boldness and courage to move things forward. However, they are rarely good at pushing what they start over the finish line.

That's where the Operator steps in. Once the dream is dreamed and the goal established, the Operator works to make the vision a reality. McKeown says of the Operator, "They'll go through a brick wall to make what needs to happen, happen. They figure out how."

Sinek wrote, "It is the magical partnership of the person with their head in the clouds and the person with their feet on the ground that creates progress."

While I never considered myself a visionary, my strengths fit McKeown's definition. On the other hand, I had minimal chops as an Operator. I had mainly spent my corporate days looking ahead, not managing the day-to-day. I had delegated most of those responsibilities, and I lacked confidence in my ability to make things happen.

Getting fired from Macy's led to a new heightened self-awareness. And it was my reliance on that self-awareness that would enable my success. While my former cocky self would have jumped into my new venture alone, I now had a clear sense of my own strengths and weaknesses. With everything on the line, I knew I needed a strong partner to compensate for my deficiencies and protect me from my often-impulsive decision-making.

I had met Rachel years earlier through Corey, a childhood friend now in the electronics business. Rachel was a young up-and-comer in the buying office at Bed Bath and Beyond, one of Corey's largest customers. Her beauty struck me first; a slender brunette with exotic almond-shaped eyes and a smile that could light up a room full of suits. She also had a remarkable intensity when it came to business. Corey complained that she was thorough, methodical, and an exceptionally tough negotiator, which took a toll on his profits. As Rachel and I came to know one another, we began to appreciate each other's approach to the business and loved to take jabs at each other's business decisions.

"Do you make your team buy all of our dogs?" she'd ask, inferring that my buyers were trying to copy her product assortment but only buying the items that didn't sell well.

"Nothing you buy would even sell if you didn't give the customer a 20% discount just for showing up," I'd answer, pointing out the ubiquitous coupons Bed Bath and Beyond slathered on their customers.

Rachel was ten years my junior, but I loved how she looked past my title and was comfortable giving me a good ribbing. We enjoyed spirited debates and commiserating over frustrations with suppliers and the retail landscape.

About a year after I met Rachel, Corey told me she had resigned from Bed Bath. He wanted to hire her, but a supplier hiring talent from a retailer was frowned upon. Retailers invest heavily to develop their people, and I've seen retaliatory actions like terminating the business of a supplier who poached an employee. The short-term benefits of hiring from a retailer might seem appealing, but most suppliers realize that the long-term consequences often outweigh the gains. To avoid a conflict, Rachel became an independent sales rep, selling products for several companies, including Corey's.

Over the next year, Rachel and I got to know each other much better, and a great friendship quickly developed. She was knowledgeable, likable, and persistent. Rachel discovered she was born to sell and really knew how to make things happen.

I was unwinding from my first marriage, and my ex and I were adjusting to our new reality as co-parents of two great boys. Somewhere along the way, friendship with Rachel turned into love, and when we married a few years later, we became true partners in business and life. She made it her mission to put my kids first and help me be the best father possible.

Starting a business with your spouse is usually a terrible idea, but Rachel and I knew we had the special sauce. We had naturally fallen into our Visionary and Operator roles. I knew where we ought to be, and Rachel knew how to get us there. I sell our dream. Rachel nails down the orders. I build the product strategy. She turns ideas into manufactured goods, shipped to arrive precisely when needed.

Her follow-up is impeccable. I do most of the talking in meetings while she takes notes, distills the key points, and hands out follow-up assignments. I move to the next thing, but she doesn't relent until all deliverables are delivered.

I tend to get impatient, but I immediately recalibrate when Rachel gives me that "look" from across the room. We are entirely comfortable offering and accepting constructive criticism. Our mutual respect defuses our defense mechanisms, allowing us to accept the feedback as intended, knowing it's shared with love.

Most days, I get to be the optimistic founder. I wake up in the morning thinking about where we need to go. She wakes up thinking about what could go wrong and how to prevent it.

We've been at each other's side almost 24/7, logging over 2 million airline miles while building our company. Though often grueling, traveling together has kept work fun.

We complement one another. Respect each other. Appreciate and admire each other. Need each other. We share a vision of success and help each other stay true to our mission.

Takeaways

PERFECTLY PAIRED

- **Success is almost always a partnership.**
  There is an African proverb, "If you want to go fast, go alone; if you want to go far, go together." Partners in the most powerful partnerships bring very different skill sets but pursue a shared vision. Rachel and I shared an understanding of how to attain success, which allowed us to fuse our complementary strengths toward a common goal.

- **Constructive criticism is a gift.**
  My dad used to tell me, "You have two ears and one mouth for a reason." When Rachel talks, I shut up and listen. She sees how my words and actions are perceived, so I take her feedback as gospel. I know she has my best interests at heart, so I accept her criticism without wasting time to defend myself. She's taught me that criticism shouldn't be destructive—it should encourage learning, build strength, heighten self-awareness, and produce breakthroughs.

12. Don't be an Entrepreneur Without an Offering

When I began telling friends about my new company, the echoes of "Congratulations! You're finally an entrepreneur!" played over and over. And each time, I'd shudder. My encounters with entrepreneurs over the years had left a lingering distaste. Flaunting their self-importance in conversations that spiraled into monologues, they'd go on and on about their products, selling, selling, selling. The incessant focus on their products overshadowed what mattered most—their *offering*.

Certainly, a product is central to an offering, but it's only a fragment. Quality, support, service, convenience, and value hold equal, if not greater, significance. A genuine offering is a confluence of these elements and more, providing a compelling reason for customers to engage with your business.

In today's digital marketplace, a simple product search yields an overwhelming number of options. The decision to purchase goes far beyond the product itself. It extends to the complete offering—the overall value proposition a company presents to win its customers.

Let me illustrate: Suppose you are searching online for a new frying pan. The array of choices is nearly endless, all serving the same primary function, with prices spanning from around 10 dollars to a few hundred. Instinctively, consumers begin to evaluate the overall offering of the listings that catch their eye. Price is important, but it isn't everything. How durable is the pan? How long will the seller stand behind it? Is the nonstick coating safe for my family? Are recipes provided? What type of utensils can I use with it? What kind of metal is it made with? Is it dishwasher-safe? Will it look good in my kitchen? Are there other matching pieces? Where's the company located? Where is the pan manufactured? When will I get it? What values does the company stand for? How will I get help if I need it? Do I trust the brand? The list goes on...

Each consumer, using their own algorithm, weighs their most important factors. After narrowing down the choices, almost inevitably, two fundamental questions are posed:

First, what is the price? Meaning, *is it a good value?*

Second, what do other consumers say in the reviews? Meaning, *can I trust you?*

A *yes* to both questions and a sale is made. *A no* to either suggests no sale, and it's back to the drawing board.

When their primary pursuit is the lowest price, the experience will unlikely *wow* the consumer. Brands that survive by selling cheap products must compromise on the elements that create a great offering, like quality and service. This short-sighted approach rarely builds an enduring and profitable business. And selling on price alone can be dispiriting for employees because it's almost impossible to do right by your customers. Moreover, it's detrimental to the environment, contributing to excessive consumption of raw materials and the release of manufacturing emissions from countless cheap products accumulating in landfills.

For months, Rachel and I brainstormed product categories in which to build our offering. After spending countless hours in all types of retail stores, our opportunity started coming into focus. The small kitchen appliance category was in dire need of a refresh. Major brands sold their products in Williams-Sonoma, Walmart, and every department store and outlet in between. Buyers were hard-pressed to create compelling reasons for consumers to shop in their stores for waffle makers, blenders, toasters, and such.

Once a locus of product innovation, the small appliances segment had become stale. The lack of innovation had created a race to the bottom on price. Which cut profitability. Which constrained investment in innovation and marketing. Which perpetuated the downward spiral.

Preparing food is a fundamental human activity, and today's kitchen, like the ancient hearth, is the heart of the place we call home. Our mission became clear—to bring enjoyment and inspiration to cooking and transform kitchens into a hub of joy and creativity.

Two groups were crucial to our success—consumers and retailers. Leveraging our extensive experience in housewares retailing, we meticulously crafted our offering. Our two-pronged strategy aimed to resonate with the younger generation of consumers and provide robust support for retailers. We were confident that we would become the best option for younger consumers whom the big brands seemed to ignore, so we turned our attention to getting placements on retail shelves.

I believed that simply eliminating friction for retailers would be the basis for a great offering, so I began to recall all the useless, wasteful resistance I had encountered on my way up the corporate ladder. Friction with bosses and coworkers. Friction with my suppliers. And friction I created for consumers by losing sight of their needs. Friction, after all, is, almost by definition, a waste of energy. And in business, friction usually means frustration for everyone.

Two contrasting scenarios played out repeatedly. On one end, there were novice entrepreneurs with exciting products, but they were shackled by a lack of understanding of retail fundamentals. In contrast, highly experienced suppliers, engulfed in complacency, had lost touch with the needs of their retailers, fostering relationships that were more contentious than productive.

These scenarios highlighted the need for a new, balanced offering to solve both frustrations. We needed to create a unique experience for retailers that would become a counterpoint to the more common relationships. To better illustrate the power of our offering, let's delve deeper into the two common scenarios mired in friction.

Let's call the first scenario:

THE PERILS OF THE NEW ENTREPRENEUR

Most start-up hopefuls are unprepared to survive their first dealings with savvy opponents. Think of *Shark Tank*. On the show, presenters expertly pitch their products but often falter when confronted with fundamental questions about their business model, growth plans, and valuation. A brutal shark-feeding fest ensues.

I've completed countless transactions with thousands of suppliers, and certain patterns have become clear. People seeking to launch a company typically fall prey to four consequential mistakes that jeopardize their chances of success:

1. **The Product Obsession:** They obsess over their product but overlook the vital importance of their offering.

2. **The Illusionary Blueprint:** They craft wildly optimistic business plans with zero connection to reality. "If I only get 3% of the population, I'll sell over ten million units!" is the sort of magical thinking you often hear from an "entrepreneur" mired deep in this delusion.

3. **The Friends-and-Family Conundrum:** With their plan in hand, they invite friends and family along on the journey—often enlisting them as investors. Of course, the folks who step up are ardent supporters who stoke the dream without offering the critical feedback needed for refinement.

4. **The Visionary Trap:** With supporters in their corner, they envision an unassailable future of entrepreneurial glory, convinced their plan is bulletproof.

The path is riddled with peril, and entrepreneurial fan culture feeds delusions. The few legendary success stories drown out the tales of failure. Think about the folks who paid $1.4 million in 2014 for their dream of a New York City taxi medallion—just before Uber changed the game.

The reality is that most start-ups barely stagger out of the starting gate and then expire quickly. Many others languish on life-support, tying up all their founders' assets and leaving them to barely make ends meet, year after year.

During my time as a retailer, trade shows were a treasure trove of innovative ideas and an opportunity to hear from the entrepreneurs behind them. On the last day of a show in Chicago, I struck up a conversation with a mother-daughter duo who abandoned their established careers in marketing to launch a company. They had a cool product, and it was apparent that they knew how to speak to the consumer. But speaking to retailers was another story.

After hearing their story, I asked, "How's the response been so far?"

"Well, we just had our best meeting!" the daughter said. "The buyer from *Bed Bath and Beyond* is placing a test order of 10,000 pieces!"

"Congratulations! How are you funding the inventory and your start-up costs?"

I was genuinely curious about how entrepreneurs approach these situations where big dollars are needed upfront.

Mom jumped in. "We don't have investors yet, so I will take a second mortgage on my home to manufacture the inventory we need. I'll pay it off as soon as the customer pays us, and we'll feed the profits back into the business."

She was thrilled with their apparent success but did not seem to recognize what a precarious situation she was putting herself into. I offered some words of warning, but they weren't about to let me bring them back to reality.

"*I hope your daughter has a comfy couch,*" I thought as we parted ways. "*You might need a place to stay by this time next year.*"

This encounter was a revelation to me. People who haven't worked with big retailers have no idea what they are in for. They can't fathom how these companies conduct business; their naivety is glaring.

The modern-day retailer has morphed into something of a landlord. When they "*buy*" products, it doesn't necessarily mean they will "*pay*" for them as one would expect—a lesson often learned too late. Buried in fine print and complex clauses, charges for markdowns, logistics, and customer returns can quickly turn profits into losses, leaving the enthusiastic entrepreneur financially battered and their dreams shattered. Maybe mom and daughter would beat the odds, but I knew how it would likely play out:

Retailer "X" says they will buy 10,000 pieces of whatever widget the entrepreneur is selling. The entrepreneur places an order with the factory and pays a 30 percent deposit, with the balance due in two to three months when the order is ready to ship.

Then, she pays a freight forwarder to get the goods into the United States, where Uncle Sam collects the import duties before the merchandise can be released from customs. Next, she pays to ship the goods from the port to their third-party warehouse to prepare them for outbound shipment to the retailer, incurring even more charges.

Only after the entrepreneur has paid, and paid, and paid, they are finally ready to make their first sale. If the retailer still comes through with their test order, which is dubious, it will be bought on open credit terms, meaning the retailer has sixty to ninety days after receiving the shipment before their payment is due. However, when a retailer tests a new supplier—often buried in the fine print—the retailer places a "credit hold" to withhold the payment for up to six months to ensure that the product sells well and return rates are not too high.

During the relationship, any product sold to a consumer and then returned to the store is typically discarded and deducted from the balance owed to the seller. If the merchandise sells at a slower-than-acceptable rate, within four to six weeks, the buyer will either mark down the goods to see if they sell at a lower price—or just mark them out of stock. Either way, the retailer charges the supplier for the loss. And it doesn't matter if the supplier protests because the retailer still holds the overdue payment. When you add the charges for returns and markdowns plus retailer-assessed fees for logistics, systems, freight to stores, marketing allowances, and more, the total could exceed 50 percent of the value of the order. If the supplier had what they thought was a healthy 30 percent gross margin, they would have suffered a significant loss. To add insult to injury, they would also have no further business with the retailer.

Let's put this into some real numbers:

Consider a scenario in which the product sold for $20 each, resulting in an apparent revenue of $200,000 from a 10,000-unit order:

Revenue: 10,000 units x $20 each = $200,000
Cost of Goods Sold: $140,000
Expected Profit at 30% Gross Margin: $60,000
Unexpected Retailer Charges:
    35% Markdown: $70,000
    8% Freight: $16,000

5% Customer Returns: $10,000
3% Miscellaneous Charges: $6,000
Total Unexpected Retailer Charges: $102,000
Actual Loss After Unexpected Charges: -$42,000

This calculation paints a stark reality: the $200,000 of "actual revenue" is whittled down to just $98,000. With a cost of goods sold of $140,000, the entrepreneur faces a staggering loss of $42,000 on a single transaction, where a profit of $60,000 was anticipated.

About one year after Mom took out the second mortgage, she'll have lost $42,000. When added to the start-up costs necessary to get that first order, she could be out a few hundred thousand dollars.

Unfortunately, this scenario is more likely to come true than the dream mom and daughter were dreaming. For most people, the first foray into retail will end in tears and most likely be their last.

But the entrepreneur won't go down without a fight. There will be countless emails, phone calls, and visits to plead their case, but the retailer's position will always be, "This is how we do business. It was in the paperwork and shouldn't have come as a surprise." These situations are brutal, so I avoided doing business with the inexperienced. Too much tedious handholding and I never want to be part of a dream crashing down.

And that brings us to my second scenario, which plays out at the other end of the spectrum:

LOSING TOUCH

Large suppliers have increasingly veered away from their retail customers' needs, creating even greater friction than buyers may experience with naive entrepreneurs.

It was my second week running Macy's Housewares business, and I was meeting my largest supplier for the first time. My large conference room could accommodate my team plus the 12 people the supplier was bringing. As the newly minted vice president, they intended to impress, and I was eager to explore how we could build a more substantial business together.

My team and I entered the meeting room and found a beautiful array of products on the table and shelves. A crisp printed-and-bound presentation was placed at each seat. I sat at the center on one side of the table, with their president facing me. As the meeting began, a glaring gap in our perspectives emerged.

"You've come on board at a great time!" their president told me. "Business is up almost 25% year-to-date, and we expect it to build to over 30% in the next three months."

I studied our business together to prepare for the meeting, so I was confused by the picture they painted.

"I'm sorry, but you said sales are up 25% year-to-date? That doesn't seem close to the numbers in our system."

He seemed a bit taken aback, but he plunged on boldly. "I'm sure of the numbers. I'm personally involved with your account. I track Macy's very closely."

My buyer pulled up our latest status report and pushed his laptop toward me.

"I'm not sure what the discrepancy is," I said, "but our system shows your business is only up 6% year-to-date. I'm not sure where your 25% figure came from."

After some awkward back and forth, he asked his people to call back to the office and check their numbers. They huddled out in the hallway, and after a few minutes, their president returned and confidently assured me his numbers were correct.

"Our business with Macy's is up 25%."

The way he boasted illuminated the situation for me.

"When you say your business with Macy's is up 25%, do you mean you shipped us 25% more than last year? Or we sold 25% more to our customers?"

"Our sales to you are up 25%. I don't know what you've sold since then." He sounded indignant.

I was astonished. In every other retail category, each supplier insisted on receiving our product sales report first thing Monday morning. They analyzed our sales even before we did. They were active participants, offering insights and strategies to improve sales of their products from week to week.

"We're in this together, so I'm a bit surprised you don't have those numbers," I told him. "Your shipments to us may be up by 25% and climbing, but our sales have only increased by 6%. And here's the real problem... Our sales are only up 6%, but our inventory is up over 20%. We've given you additional support, but it hasn't translated into the sales growth I would expect. If you continue to ship large increases and our sales don't increase at the same rate, the next time we meet, we'll have an unpleasant conversation about you taking goods back or paying to promote them."

The meeting ended on an awkward note. They had no interest in being active participants in running our mutual business. I assumed it was an anomaly, but versions of that scenario played out repeatedly with different suppliers. Housewares suppliers didn't seem to comprehend the pressures we faced as retailers. Learning as much as possible about how, why, and where their products were selling or not selling should have been as important to them as it was to us, but they just didn't get it.

CREATE A NECESSARY OFFERING

Since the early days of commerce, the wholesaler–retailer relationship has been punctuated by tension. The traditional model prioritizes individual gains, often at the other party's expense, while the consumer is often overlooked. I began formulating our mission to change that paradigm. We would be a wholesaler with a new approach and a company culture emphasizing collaboration and shared success. Our aim would be symbiotic relationships with our retailers where prioritizing their needs would bolster our business. We would never, ever lose sight of the customer. In our new paradigm, everyone wins.

During my time in retail, I had a front-row seat to the deterioration of the retailer-supplier relationship. The priorities of retailers and suppliers are often in opposition. Retailers seek advantages over their retail competitors. Suppliers try to maintain a level playing field, wary of appearing to favor one customer over another. Retailers want precisely what they need when they need it; suppliers need to sell what they have, whether those products are meeting sales thresholds or not. Retailers negotiate aggressively for the lowest price possible to pad their margins. Suppliers try for the highest price they can get to pad their margins.

By 2010, when I launched StoreBound, the typical retailer-supplier relationship was like two people in a canoe, facing each other and paddling in opposite directions. No one was getting where they wanted to go.

I knew that our expertise in retail and our empathy for the buyers—Rachel and I had been there—was something that could set our company apart. I didn't know what products we would be selling, but I began the crucial step of defining our offering. I wanted our company and our customers to paddle in the same direction to make progress together. Our success would hinge on their success. Their goals had to be our goals. I wanted to forge customer relationships 180 degrees from the norm.

I knew buyers would welcome our retail expertise if we used it to make their lives easier. Even before we had the first product to sell, the pitch for our offering began to take shape. This is how it went:

"We've sat in your chair, and we understand your challenges. We've done business with all your suppliers, so we know that every time your phone rings or you get an email, your day gets worse. We are going to

do the opposite. We may be new, but we know exactly what we're doing. Our goal is to help you achieve your goals. Your success will be our success, and we'll prove that to you every day."

We would go beyond selling them superb products. We would apply our expertise to help solve their problems. We would do the heavy lifting for our retailers, develop compelling proposals for increasing their sales, and help them execute every step of the way. And if things didn't go as expected, we would be there to make it right. We would even step in to help solve problems caused by other suppliers.

Developing a great product line would be the easy part. The true value of our offering was our awareness that nothing is really, finally sold until the product is in the hands or in the home of a consumer who loves it, knows they got a fair deal, and will show loyalty to the retailer and our brand.

Our offering was strong. It was time to prepare to do business.

Takeaways
DON'T BE AN ENTREPRENEUR WITHOUT AN OFFERING

- **Your customers' business is your business.** Henry Ford said, "Coming together is a beginning, staying together is progress, and working together is success." Ford's wisdom underscored my ambition to prove the potential of a symbiotic relationship between wholesalers and retailers.

  With firsthand experience of the day-to-day hurdles, we crafted our company identity not just as a vendor but as a genuine ally to our retailers. Our business across the entire retail spectrum gave us a broader vantage point than any of our individual retailers. Combining thought leadership with our broader perspective, we earned trust and offered vital insights to the retailers supporting our business. Our promise was their success. It clearly resonated, and many bought in at the outset.

- **Your buyers aren't customers; they're partners.** There's always room for improvement in buyer-seller relationships. Ask questions, listen to the answers, and discover new ways to raise the bar. By demonstrating unwavering reliability and adding value, we would transform our buyers into steadfast champions, with their loyalty propelling our new business toward sustained success.

- **A great offering adds value to a great product.**
  An egg cooker was one of our first best-selling products. My initial sales pitch focused on everything it can do—cook up to six eggs at a time, hard-boil, soft-boil, medium-boil, poach eggs, make omelets, even steam fish or veggies. Plus, it's cute, compact, and all its accessories store neatly inside. In other words, it does precisely what all the other egg cookers on the market do.

  After hearing my sales pitch, our head of marketing connected the product to our offering in an eye-opening way: "We're not selling an egg cooker like so many competing brands—we're offering *healthy breakfast, fast.*"

  Ours is more expensive than most competitors, but our offering makes us the best value. For our retailers, the offering includes higher margins and meticulously designed packaging that acts like a salesperson on their understaffed selling floors. Our packages are expensive to design and produce, but they increase our sales productivity, which aligns with our goal of improving our retailers' results.

  For the consumer, our "Healthy Breakfast in a Dash" offering starts with compelling packaging that includes our USA customer service phone number in case they have questions before they purchase. When the consumer gets the product home, they'll find a full-color instruction manual, a quick-start guide, recipes explicitly developed for the product, and links to videos to help them get the most from their purchase. And with our high-quality materials and manufacturing, the product will perform for years and years. The extra effort is all about winning the hearts of our customers. And that's what building brand loyalty is all about.

13. From Vision to Venture

Three things need to happen before a start-up can become a real, live business:
1. Connecting with prospective customers.
2. Presenting them with a compelling offering.
3. Understanding how to transact business.

Unlike most new entrepreneurs, Rachel and I were not newcomers. We arrived on the scene, fully prepared, recognizing how to convert our vision into a stream of revenue.

1) CUSTOMERS

Establishing close relationships with influential decision-makers in an industry can take years, but Rachel and I had a head start. Our collective Rolodex was packed with opportunities. The people we hoped to call our customers were often friends and former colleagues. We spoke their language and understood the marketplace—ours and theirs—so we could navigate effectively without the steep learning curve.

Our approach was purposeful. We knew which retailers could build our brand equity by displaying our products beautifully and marketing them intelligently, versus those who might stack them in piles and run discounts. We knew where we wanted to be.

Even though we were still working on the products, what we were offering was becoming crystal clear: a better way to do business. In retrospect, our offering was akin to what made Amazon a titan of the retail landscape. We were going to make buying and selling easy for everyone.

Retailers wanted the same thing we did—friction-free relationships. Transactions that would inspire customer loyalty—and in some instances, we learned, devotion. Our reputations enabled us to get appointments with the right buyers quickly and our offering allowed us to immediately connect, stirring the curiosity of potential buyers.

2) PRODUCTS

Our goal was to creatively disrupt a lethargic small appliance business, but that would take time, and it wouldn't be cheap. Complex electrical products take time to develop. We needed a shortcut to get into business and start generating revenue ASAP.

Our longstanding relationships with manufacturers and international brands provided an avenue, allowing immediate access to products we could distribute in the United States. These products were already developed and didn't demand the scale of investment required to design and develop our own line. It was the shortcut we needed to get the company off the ground.

These products were the key to our top objective—to obtain a vendor number with every key retailer. You need a vendor number to do business. No ifs or buts. Getting it can take six months or longer. Without it, a buyer can't place an order with you, no matter how badly they want to buy your products. By securing these vendor numbers, we could begin generating revenue while developing our future product line.

3) GOING TRANSACTIONAL

In my last year at Macy's, my buyers purchased over $3 billion of merchandise from over 2,000 suppliers. I had no idea where most of the products originated or how they got to where they needed to go. When we founded the company, we needed to learn everything about that basic, fundamental, rubber-meets-the-road side of the business.

I had minimal experience on the operations side, and the financial requirements of running a small business were also new to me. Sure, I knew how all the numbers worked together, but I had never been responsible for managing the money. The billions of dollars I "handled" over the years were just numbers on reports. When it's your own money, it's different.

In addition to learning operations and financial management, I had to manage a nonstop stream of systems issues, all demanding decisions yesterday. How do I implement an accounting or ERP system? Which government certifications or registrations were necessary? How would we deal with quality control on goods produced halfway around the world? What insurance would we need? What about hedging currency?

To make informed decisions, I needed expertise in plenty of areas I was unfamiliar with. But if I dove deep into operations, systems, and finance, I would have less time to focus on my product development, sales, and marketing strengths.

Rachel and I discussed the situation and agreed we needed to hire outsourced talent to back us up in the areas where we lacked expertise. Our immense network would enable us to find the right service providers, allowing us to keep our focus on sales, products, and marketing.

We were clear about one thing—we were outsourcing to people, not companies. We looked past websites and presentations and interviewed each service provider as though they were applying to become members of our team. We sought ambitious problem-solvers who mirrored our values and team spirit.

Shortly after launching, we signed contracts with a distribution and logistics provider, an international freight forwarder, a business systems provider, and an overseas supply chain and quality control organization. The investment in these contracts was substantial, and while we could have managed certain aspects ourselves for much less, we understood that any momentary savings could potentially derail us. Rachel and I needed to keep our focus on sales and marketing to drive the top-line growth of the business. Over a decade later, these partnerships remain intact.

Our strategy to outsource operations was the right decision, which became very clear to us one warm afternoon in Arkansas. We were in year three of our business. After about ten trips to Bentonville to pitch products to Sam's Club, we finally broke through. Along the way, we developed mutual respect with Ryan, the young buyer who oversaw our category. Ryan had put us through our paces. He was tough on our business model. He was tough on our presentations. He was tough on our products. And when the time came, he was a tough negotiator. But we were determined to prove we would become a strong supplier in their clubs. When he finally gave us the opportunity, it was more than a small test. We would have two pallet positions in almost 500 clubs for two months. This was huge.

I remember that day vividly. Rachel and I returned to our rental car to review our notes and start the follow-up before heading back to the airport.

Supplier parking at Sam's headquarters is limited, so we moved to a remote lot where we parked right next to a lone green shipping container. We opened our laptops and started working through the next steps to push a deal forward. At some point, I glanced out the window and stared at the shipping container just sitting there, alone in a parking lot. It looked like it had been there a while, too. It looked lost.

I started to laugh. "This is totally something we would do," I said to Rachel.

"What?"

"Picture this. We get our first order from Sam's Club, and we still have no idea what we're doing. We get the goods made overseas. When our freight company is doing the paperwork, they ask us for the shipping address. We have no clue, so we Google it and then send them Sam's headquarters address. A month later, when the container should arrive at their distribution center, it's dropped off in their parking lot. This parking lot. And there it sits."

"We're so clueless," Rachel said, shaking her head and laughing.

Giddiness about the opportunity quickly turned to anxiety as we realized we had no idea how to ship products to Sam's Club. We needed to know immediately because Sam's needed correct and final pricing right away, which was impossible for us to offer without understanding all their shipping requirements.

We called Ryan's office, and his assistant instructed us to download their "Routing Guide" and "Standards Manual" from the vendor portal on the web. We opened two PDFs, each hundreds of pages in length. We struggled to absorb them, still in the parking lot, but the requirements seemed different than those of every other retailer we were shipping to. What kind of pallets did we need to use? We couldn't make heads or tails of how to build the pallets to the specs they wanted. Did the maximum height of the pallet include the actual pallet? Could our boxes extend a couple of inches over the edge of the pallet? What was the maximum weight per pallet?

After nearly an hour of trying to sort this out in the rental car in the parking lot in Arkansas, we called our pal Cheryl, who handled our goods at the third-party warehouse we had contracted.

"Cheryl!"

"Evan!"

"Do you know how to ship products to Sam's Club?"

"We do it all the time."

"That's great. Seriously. Excellent. Trying to make sense of this was freaking me out. Okay, we have two different products Sam's Club wants to buy. So, we're trying to make sense of how to configure the pallet—we've downloaded their routing guide and standards manual, and Rachel's here with me, and we've started to go through them, and we have some concerns. First, which pallets do we need to use--"

"Evan," Cheryl said.

"--and do you load the pallet at the warehouse or the factory? And it seems there are options—"

"Evan, listen-"

"--but if it's done at the factory-"

"EVAN!" Cheryl barked.

I caught myself. "Uh, yes?"

"Evan, we ship Sam's all the time. We just need to know the products they're buying. We'll build your pallets to their exact standards. You'll have a couple of choices. The only decision you'll need to make is which displays your products better."

"Really?

"Really."

"This is such a relief," I whispered.

"I'll email you all the details!" Rachel chimed in.

"Perfect," said Cheryl. "Congratulations, by the way. And listen, you guys worry about the selling. We'll handle getting your stuff where it needs to go and how it needs to get there."

Our sighs of relief reverberated off the lone shipping container next to our car. Rachel and I would have spent days trying to figure out arcane shipping details. We'd probably have made costly mistakes. We would never get it done the way Cheryl could get it done.

Variations of that scene played out repeatedly, reaffirming the wisdom of hiring outside expertise where our expertise was lacking. With the right partners, we could devote all our efforts to what we were very good at—sales and marketing, which were critical to our success.

Takeaways
FROM VISION TO VENTURE

- **Become an industry expert before you become an entrepreneur.**
  My corporate journey was akin to earning a Ph.D. in retail. However, rather than shelling out tuition year after year, I was compensated generously. I learned hands-on and made nearly every mistake that could be made. And I did it on someone else's dime!

  Understanding a marketplace is paramount before diving in as an entrepreneur. My expertise in the Housewares sector was hard-earned. I'd been a major customer of every supplier, so I was well-versed with our competitors and intimately familiar with their strengths, weaknesses, and selling tactics. I also had a deep understanding of consumer preferences and knew what the big brands weren't offering. I was confident we could develop great products to fill those gaps.

- **You can't transact if you can't transact.**
  Many aspiring entrepreneurs tried to sell me something before they were equipped to transact business. Several times, I tried to buy their products, only to discover they had no idea how to handle a purchase order. Once they wasted my time, they wouldn't get a second chance.

Pre-transactional businesses are everywhere at trade shows, so I began weeding out these suppliers by asking questions like, "Are you on EDI?" EDI is the universal computer system connecting retailers and suppliers. The only way to receive an order from a large retailer is via EDI. The only way to invoice that retailer is via EDI. Deploying the system can take thousands of dollars and several months. But if you're trying to sell to a large retailer, and you're not on EDI—well, it's just not going to happen.

- **You don't have to know it all.**
Yes, you need to be an expert in your industry, but that doesn't mean you have to be proficient in everything. Modern business is complex, and success isn't about knowing how to perform every function; it's about understanding where and when to seek outside expertise. Align with providers adept at navigating the areas you don't know. Make it personal. Interview the people who will be handling your business. Check references. Find out what happens when things go wrong and who will fix it. Nurture these relationships and know whom to call when things go sideways because, at some point, they most certainly will.

14. Money Doesn't Grow on Trees

Rachel and I lived in the heart of the Financial District in New York City. Eighty percent of the world's money flows through the neighborhood every single day. You can almost feel it pulsing through the narrow arteries of downtown Manhattan.

When I told friends in finance that I planned to start my own company, people seemed to think my timing was terrific.

"It's an incredible time to go after funding, Evan!"

"There's a giant overhang out there—way more money than good places to invest it!"

"People will be throwing millions at you."

Okay! I liked the sound of people throwing millions at me. So, I put together a business plan and booked some meetings. My financial projections were strong. Our strategy made sense. I had a great track record and lots of hands-on experience in the industry. Plus, I was offering something unique and much-needed in the market I hoped to break into.

When I started making my way around the neighborhood, I met with private equity companies to gauge the market's temperature. My very first meeting was with four people from a multi-billion-dollar firm. I was in the middle of what I thought was a concise and compelling overview of my background and business plan when the big cheese in the room cut me off.

"What's your exit strategy?" he demanded.

"Excuse me?" I didn't want to be rude, but an *exit* strategy was the last thing I'd considered. "Maybe I wasn't clear. I'm working on my *entrance* strategy."

Wrong answer. Uncomfortable silence. Finally, the guy sitting next to the big boss spoke up. "Uh, that's great, Evan, but we're more interested in how we get out and recoup our investment."

Okay. I left that meeting knowing these were not my people. I'm sure the feeling was mutual. No problem. Plenty of fish in the sea.

My next meeting was with a firm that had just completed an $800 million raise for their new fund. I heard they were eagerly looking for investment opportunities. And here I was, standing at the front of the line.

This time, I opened with an even more concise and to-the-point summary of my background and the opportunity I was presenting. And once again, I was interrupted. These private equity guys really believed that time was money, and they weren't about to let me waste theirs.

"You have no revenue or assets," their CFO said. "How would we even begin to assign a valuation to calculate an offer?"

Translation: Get out of my conference room.

The third meeting was with a more prominent firm. Their team looked young and dynamic. Great, I thought, my kind of people: positive, enthusiastic, dedicated.

It seemed I had it right. Things were going great. By which, I mean for the first time, they were attentive to my pitch and let me finish. They seemed genuinely interested and asked astute questions. They seemed to have taken the bait and run with the hook. But then came the sinker.

"This sounds exactly like Quirky," said the guy I had thought was getting it.

Quirky was a crowd-sourced product innovation company rumored to have just raised $100 million in financing. I was nothing like Quirky. I didn't believe in their model and needed them to understand that.

"Our model is the opposite of Quirky in almost every aspect," I said. "They work with inventors transparently on the internet. We will work privately, under a nondisclosure agreement, and with a financial model that allows us to achieve a compelling retail price point for each product."

"Go on," the CEO said. He looked interested.

So, I ran with it. "Quirky works with a small army of inventors, and they involve an even larger public group to develop the products in an open forum. Everyone can see their product concepts long before they are commercialized. They also must reserve a significant portion of their sales revenue to pay everyone who worked on the development, which could be hundreds of people. That ultimately means an inflated retail price and lower sales. The retail industry can't metabolize the high prices or the necessary margin concessions. We'll work quickly, but the first time the public or competitors see our product, it will already be in retail stores."

"Still sounds kinda like Quirky to me," an analyst said, shooting me a snarky grin from the far end of the table.

Now I was annoyed. "Quirky uses community transparency as a key aspect of their model. It allows anyone in the industry to view their product forums to gain as much inspiration as they would like. The designs will be in the public domain before patents can be filed. Knockoffs will land in the market before the real thing. Their model is highly flawed. We won't be anything like Quirky."

"Quirky raised nearly $100 million in private equity," the snarky guy said.

"Quirky's "crowd-sourcing" model gets a lot of buzz. Our process may not be as sexy, but it will produce far better results."

The room brooded on that for a while.

"I do think you have something here," said the CEO. "How does this sound? We'd put $1 million of equity into the business to get you started, and we can facilitate a loan of up to, say, $10 million if sales and revenue approach your year-three projections. Since you are pre-revenue, we need to own a majority of the shares."

Huh? If I wanted to build a company for somebody else, I'd go back to the corporate world and take another big job with another big salary. I'd have collected my stock options without worrying about the risk.

The CEO wished me luck and asked me to stay in touch.

After three more meetings and three more comparisons to Quirky, it became clear that Plan A—seeking a private equity investor—was not a successful strategy, overhang or no overhang. The problem was I had not yet built anything of value, so I wasn't a candidate for investment under acceptable terms. And if one more analyst asked me what my *exit strategy* was, I would not be held responsible for my answer.

I needed Plan B, maybe even a Plan C.

The night after our last meeting, Rachel and I went out to dinner. She was in a somber mood after the resounding belly flop on Wall Street and gave me a questioning look when I ordered a bottle of champagne.

"Seriously? What are we celebrating, exactly? Do tell."

"You'll see."

Maybe she was thinking—or hoping—that I'd gone and gotten my job at Macy's back.

Our waiter returned with the champagne. He carefully twisted off the basket, pulled out the cork with a great popping sound, poured us each a glass, and then set the bottle in a bucket next to the table.

I held up my glass.

"Sitting with those PE guys, I had a revelation. Bringing investors on too early could be worse than having no investors at all. I was so focused on the chase that I ignored how detrimental it would have been for us to make a deal. We own 100% of the company, and we're in control of our destiny."

"To StoreBound and to us," Rachel said, clinking her glass against mine.

Maybe she still thought it was crazy to celebrate what felt like a failure, but Rachel believes in me 100 percent.

The following day, with my hopes of finding an investor dashed, I stood alone in my bathroom feeling my confidence shaken. My hands rested on the cold vanity as I gazed at myself in the mirror.

"Can you do this?" I asked.

The guy in the mirror didn't look convinced. He knew the venture I was embarking on would be completely different than anything I had done before.

As a corporate executive, I underwent an intensive review process each year. Sales and profitability carried the most weight. On the review form, they fall into the category marked **"GETS RESULTS."** Year after year, I **GOT RESULTS**. But did I? Were those results mine? Or did they rightfully belong to my team? To the associates in the stores? Or my suppliers? Or to the momentum in the categories themselves? How could I claim them as my own? My feeling of doubt was palpable as I stared myself down in the mirror.

As I took in the worried face in the mirror, I started to think clearly. I've seen this movie before. The football team is in the locker room at halftime, down by two touchdowns, feeling dejected, and on the brink of losing the championship.

It wasn't halftime of a game, though. It was the halftime of my career. When the second half started, there would be new opponents and new rules of the game. I had no team to rely on and no staff to delegate to. It was 100% on Rachel and me to deliver the results. We needed to execute a new game plan to persuade buyers that they needed what we were selling.

As I envisioned what it would take, I grew more and more confident. Pretty soon, I saw what I was looking for —the man in the mirror had that slight smirk. The eyes had that familiar fire. It was my game face, and it was *on*. I knew we had everything it would take to win in the second half.

It was time to turn my attention to *"getting results"* once again.

Takeaways
MONEY DOESN'T GROW ON TREES

- **Don't get caught in the thrill of the chase.**
  While ambition is the fuel that propels businesses forward, unchecked ambition, without genuine understanding, can lead to fatal victories.

  When I heard that investors would be "throwing money at me," I locked in on the prize. The chase was on! Blinded by the allure of start-up capital, I couldn't see that taking on an investor might mean giving up control. Or even worse, inviting the wrong people into our company and giving them carte blanche to make our lives miserable.

  Those private equity meetings revealed what we should have known—there is no easy money. There are always tradeoffs, and a very clear understanding of those tradeoffs is crucial before getting swept up in the chase. Disengaging from the chase for private equity was a transformative moment. It strengthened our resolve and focused us on building the business on our own terms, which paid long-term dividends.

- **Overconfidence creates blind spots.**
  Shortly after we launched the company, industry trade journals penned flattering articles about our fresh approach to rapid product innovation.

The day after a prominent article ran, I received a lavish gift basket. Nestled in the assortment was a note: "Congratulations on your new innovative business model," signed, "Your Friends at Quirky."

The underlying tone was unmistakable, suggesting, "We know you are planning to copy our business."

The folks at Quirky thought so highly of their model that they assumed I would attempt to replicate it. Their arrogance blinded them from seeing StoreBound as a different and superior concept. And while they were busy feeling threatened, they failed to see that their own business was on shaky ground.

On September 22, 2015, Steve Lohr from the New York Times wrote, "Quirky, an ambitious crowd-sourced invention start-up, which raised $185 million from investors that included General Electric and leading venture capital firms, filed for bankruptcy on Tuesday."

Once a darling of the investment community, Quirky's demise underscored the importance of recognizing and staying open-minded to the intricacies of different business models. We were always kicking the tires of other models to ensure that we were built to last. We believed that a lean, agile organization, loaded with creativity and focused on a winning hearts mission, would outperform the competition and endure the inevitable ups and downs of the market.

15. From Red-Eyes to Realizations

A week after realizing Wall Street wasn't the right path, I was on a plane headed to the West Coast for my very first sales call. I was meeting with the Housewares buyer for Gottschalks, a small department store chain based in Fresno. They were a hyper-local franchise with about 58 stores across 6 Western states. Gottschalks, like Mervyn's, Gump's, and many other small and beloved local chains, has since been liquidated. They could not compete with big boxes or larger consolidated chains of department stores.

I had developed a friendly rapport with Wendy, the Housewares Buyer at Gottschalks. I convinced her to give me an appointment and eagerly anticipated meeting her in person. My alarm went off at 3:30 a.m. I was not exactly bright-eyed and bushy-tailed on my way to the airport to catch the day's first flight out of JFK, but I figured I'd manage a few more hours of sleep on the plane.

I rolled my giant bag to the check-in counter, put it on the scale, and paid my first salesperson tax—$50 because it was over 50 pounds. I was annoyed but told myself it was still cheaper than shipping the samples out ahead of time.

I was too hyped up to sleep on the flight. I kept going over my presentation. I made a few changes and planned to stop at Kinko's to print the updates on my way to the meeting.

We touched down right on time. After a short wait at baggage claim, my gigantic suitcase slid onto the carousel with a ponderous thud. I wrestled it off the conveyor and headed to the rental car shuttle. Everything so far was going off without a hitch.

My name was on the board, and my car was waiting in its numbered stall. The trunk was already open. I felt like the happy customer in a Hertz commercial. I punched the address into the built-in GPS, a special feature in those days, and was on my way.

Three hours later, I rolled into Fresno. My first stop was the local Gottschalks, where I took myself on a walk-through. I wanted to be familiar with their assortment of products before the meeting. I made a few mental notes, then hopped to Kinko's to print my updated deck. I still had a few minutes to grab a snack, but I wasn't hungry. I had butterflies. I couldn't remember the last time I'd felt such anxious anticipation. I knew my presentation was solid and I could deliver it well—but this sales call mattered so much.

I arrived at their corporate offices. Game time. I wrestled my sample case from the trunk and started toward the entrance. I was rolling the sample case in front of me when it hit a concrete parking block. The wheels stopped, sending the case down with a thud. I tumbled over it, bouncing off the case and landing on the hot, sticky asphalt.

Fortunately, the only thing that fractured was my composure. Whatever. I wasn't bleeding and my clothes weren't torn. I looked almost as good as new, and the lot was empty—no gawking spectators. I got up, dusted myself off, and cautiously headed to the receptionist, where I signed in.

"I'm scheduled to meet with Wendy, the Housewares Buyer," I said, handing over my business card.

"Have a seat, and I'll let her know you're here."

After about a 15-minute wait, Wendy's Assistant Buyer, Samantha, came out and introduced herself.

"I am so sorry," she said over her shoulder as we walked down a hallway toward the conference room she had booked. "Something came up, and Wendy can't make the meeting. But don't worry. I'll take good notes."

I couldn't believe it. I had gotten up at 3:30 a.m. to fly economy to San Francisco, to drive to Fresno, to meet with Wendy—and she'd sent her assistant instead?

And I shouldn't worry because the assistant would be *taking good notes?*

The corporate executive in me would have seriously acted out at this point.

The start-up guy, however, was learning to look at things a little differently. For one thing, I felt empathy for Samantha, who had to deliver the bad news for Wendy. She had been put in a tough spot, so I made a real effort to put her at ease. None of this was her fault.

I told Samantha a story about my early days in retail when my buyer had double-booked meetings and made me cover one for her. I fell in love with the product line and convinced my buyer to test some of their styles. They went on to become the best-performing new brand in our area.

Hint. Hint.

Samantha told me about their business, and I told her about starting the company and why I'd chosen this product category. Then I walked through my presentation.

Sam was tough. She reviewed the products and explained why they probably wouldn't perform well for her stores. I was a little unnerved, listening to someone with less than two years of retail experience tell me I had it all wrong. But I took it with a smile. And once I had recovered from the shock of Samantha not being absolutely smitten with my wonderful products, I tried some respectful logic. I reminded her I was familiar with her market, having previously worked with stores all across the region—many in the same locations as hers. I politely presented market research that we had done that strongly suggested her stores would do well with our products.

Sam admitted the intel was intriguing and seemed willing to reconsider. Despite the hard time she had given me, I liked her from the outset. Sam handled herself exceptionally well for someone relatively new to the business. When the meeting concluded, she promised to present everything we had covered to Wendy and hoped her boss would like it.

I'd hoped to come out of there with a commitment, but transforming Samantha's doubts into what sounded like serious interest would have to do for now. I got back into my rental for the three-hour drive back to San Francisco, took a deep breath, and looked in the rearview mirror. The guy looking back at me didn't look uncertain anymore. I had made it through my first sales call and still had my game face on. That was going to have to be good enough for now.

Calling a brand-new business a start-up makes it sound like all you do is turn a key or press a fob, and the motor starts humming.

Not even close.

Starting up was going to be a journey. I was determined to make it a successful one, but it wasn't going to happen all at once, and it might never happen in Fresno. I needed to cultivate a level of patience that I never had time to develop in the go-go-go corporate world.

Other people who had achieved my level of corporate success might have bailed after the two weeks I just had— getting turned down by every investor, schlepping samples across the country, falling in a parking lot, trying to convince a junior person in a small company that I knew what I was talking about, then leaving the meeting that had been inconclusive, at best, to drive three hours back to the airport to lug my overweight samples back across the country on a red-eye flight. It would have been enough to send most people in my position racing back to the comforts of the executive floor. Instead, I was looking forward to the next challenge. My eyes were on the prize.

I got to the airport in good time, dropped off the rental, and caught the red-eye home, where I had a long shower, a quick nap, then got a few hours of work done. That afternoon, I headed to the suburban elementary school on Long Island to pick up my kids. If I'd still been in the corporate world, I would have taken the red-eye—business class, not economy, then headed straight to the office for a full day, and somebody else would have picked up my kids. But as a single dad, divorced for a few years, I seized every opportunity to show up for them. On my way to their school, my phone rang.

"Evan, it's Sam from Gottschalks."

"Hey, Sam."

"Made it home okay?"

"Sure did."

"Thanks again for coming all the way out here. Wendy is on the line too."

"Hi Evan," Wendy said.

"Hey, Wendy."

"I'm so sorry I missed you yesterday. Sam showed me your presentation, and we love what you're developing."

Moments later, we were discussing the details of doing business together. We were still hammering out the next steps as I pulled into the pickup line at school. The call ended just as my little guys saw me and ran to the car. There was no better feeling than seeing their giant smiles, beyond excited to see Daddy doing pickup.

And Gottschalks had just become our first customer. So we were on our way.

Takeaways
FROM RED-EYES TO REALIZATIONS

- **When humility triumphs over ego, you move closer to success.**
  Countless times during my childhood, when I'd start to do something impulsive, my dad would say, "Nothing good is going to come of that." Whether jumping off a ledge, running in a store, or bothering my brother, he was always right. And when nothing good can come of it, only a fool would do it.

  As a kid, it saved me from trouble or injury, but now, my dad's voice suppressed the impulses that would have derailed my pursuit of success. Whenever a customer talked down to me or told me things that weren't true, I resisted the urge to speak my mind. Getting into an unnecessary conflict with the same people I counted on for progress would have sabotaged my goals, so instead, I acted like the adult in the room: the wise, temperate, thoughtful, considerate adult, determined to develop the relationship, not burn it down.

- **Discover true success in simple moments.**
  For years, I chased a vision of what I imagined success looked like. The seat at the head of the boardroom table. Leading the quarterly earnings call with the investment community. The most lucrative compensation package. Stock options out the wazoo. My face on the cover of the annual report.

  The moment I saw the delight on my kids' faces in the pickup line outside their school, I knew I'd had it all wrong. Success was owning my calendar. Working with people I chose. Building something. Showing up for my kids.

16. Choose Discipline Over Disarray

Business was beginning to take off, and Rachel and I were in Italy to meet with a manufacturer—but not before enjoying our first 24-hour vacation in two years.

It couldn't have come at a better time. After two years of working around the clock, positive cash flow seemed finally within reach. We felt entitled to a brief respite in luxury.

Asolo is in Italy's Veneto region and one of those beautiful, not-well-known places—a medieval town with narrow cobblestone streets and a history stretching back to the 800s. We arrived on a beautiful afternoon. Just being in Asolo delivered a change in perspective.

The start-up stage had been stressful. We hadn't yet seen dollar one in profit. Instead, we were hemorrhaging cash by hiring designers, renting office space, buying inventory, and now traveling to Europe to meet new manufacturers and potential customers. Every time I checked our bank balance, we'd hit a new low.

I wasn't alarmed, though. Not yet. We had known we would have to spend money to get our venture off the ground.

Our financial plan was solid, although with so much going on during the start-up phase, I hadn't revisited it in months.

We were staying in a beautiful hotel, the Villa Cipriani. Our room looked out over the hills, with spires of medieval towns in the distance. The gardens surrounding the hotel had rustic stone walls, flagstone paths, and flowers in full bloom. The fruit trees and a beautifully tended garden supplied the hotel's restaurant.

That night, we dressed up for dinner. The staff was so attentive and kind that we felt like we had the dining room to ourselves—and it was off-season, so we nearly did. The chef was delighted to have appreciative people to cook for, and the staff plied us with wine as we enjoyed course after course of a delightful meal. Dinner took four hours. We laughed and reminisced about everything that had led us to this wonderful night, nearly our last stop on the way to becoming successful business owners. The allure of Italy was undeniable; from its wine and cuisine to its warm-hearted people, it was impossible not to fall in love.

Heading back to our room, each carrying a last glass of wine, we stopped, sat down on an old stone wall, and looked out over the hills in the moonlight. How lucky we were to have a night like this! To be building our own company and our future free of the nagging pressures of corporate life. It was the perfect end to a magical night.

A few hours later, I came awake suddenly in our hotel room. I sat up in bed, breathing hard. I felt overwhelmed with anxiety and dread. My heart was pounding. I felt like I was drowning.

I was convinced that I had just checked the balance on our checking account and that somehow, in the hours since we had gone to sleep, our company had burned through all its remaining cash.

Without waking Rachel, I swung my legs down and sat on the edge of the bed. What should I do now? Call the office and shut everything down? Acknowledge the truth:

that our venture was a complete disaster, profitability an illusion?

How had we gotten ourselves here? What had I been thinking? What about my children, whose future I had so foolishly gambled? And what would I tell our team, those dedicated, hopelessly naïve people I'd persuaded to join us? How had all our balances turned negative overnight? Why hadn't I been on top of it? How had I lost track of our financials?

For a few seconds, rationality struggled to assert itself. Could this be a dream?

No. No way. I was wide awake in a hotel room in Italy. I'd never been so awake! My fear was like a wild animal that had fled its cage.

My thinking was circular and out of control. Rationality was out the window.

Was this a panic attack?

No way, I'd been a firefighter; I don't do panic. This was real.

Whatever I'd been hiding from up until now needed to be faced.

Rachel was sleeping so peacefully. I couldn't bring myself to wake her with the awful news of impending disaster. We had crashed and burned, and it was all my fault. We had to get home. Right away. Today. Book a flight. Start looking for a job. Now. Immediately.

Though I was still deep in the spin, part of me knew I had to ground myself in reality. Following that instinct, I grabbed my laptop, pulled on a bathrobe, and left the room as quietly as possible, heading out to the garden.

Under the stars, I started to feel my breathing return to normal. I began to feel almost myself. This was just a problem I had to solve, right? And I knew how to solve problems.

What had changed between last night, when everything seemed perfect, and this morning, with the world closing in around me? I needed to find out.

Sitting in a lounge chair under a lemon tree, I pulled up our business plan. The landscape was aglow with dawn, but I barely noticed. I quickly updated our financial position, including current expense rates, bank account balance, and the date we projected to become revenue-positive. I reviewed sales assumptions and made a few changes.

As I worked through the forecast, I suddenly remembered a phone call that had come in the middle of the night. Someone had called me at the hotel to tell me our credit card balance exceeded our limit, and I needed to pay in full immediately. I knew this was ridiculous. I logged into American Express and saw the card was recently paid. What a relief!

Sitting in the garden, logic began to return. I was stepping out from one of the most realistic nightmares I had ever experienced. There had been no phone call from American Express. There was no impending doom. The dream had provoked the panic attack—it had all seemed so vividly real.

I've always been rational when it comes to business. I never persuaded myself that things were going according to plan when they weren't. When things did go wrong, I did not waste energy on excuses; I focused on fixing the problem. And the experience I had just highlighted a fundamental problem: I didn't have my arms around our financials. Some part of me had known this, and that had left me vulnerable. A combination of exhaustion, exhilaration, and excessive wine did the rest. Had I been on top of our numbers, I would have dismissed my fears and gone back to sleep.

That morning in the garden was a turning point. I vowed that I would never again be in a position where I didn't have a solid grip on our financial condition. In the corporate world, I'd always taken pride in knowing exactly where my business stood at any given time. In a big company, knowing the numbers is an essential survival skill. People are always asking, and if you can't provide clear and accurate information on the spot, they'll start losing confidence in you.

Now that I was my own boss, with no one to report to, I had lost my close grip on the financials. I knew the direction but not the details. I'd gone nearly a year without a single financial meeting because there was no finance team. Not knowing the numbers was unsettling, even a little humiliating, though it was overshadowed by the relief I felt knowing that we were fine. StoreBound would live to see another day.

With her typical perfect timing, Rachel appeared in the garden with her beautiful, reassuring smile. She didn't ask how long I'd been sitting there in my bathrobe, or what I was doing on the computer. I certainly didn't volunteer the truth. I shut the laptop and returned to our room to get dressed then met Rachel in the restaurant. The coffee was exactly what I needed. The rolls were fresh, the marmalade made from oranges grown on the trees outside, and the eggs were from chickens living adventurous and fulfilling lives.

"Evan, why did you get up so early? What were you doing out there?"

"Oh, I couldn't sleep. Figured I might as well do some work, and I didn't want to wake you.

"Is everything okay?"

"Of course."

And everything *was* okay. By then, I felt lucid and re-energized. And determined never to let the details of our financial condition slip out of my grasp again.

A growing business lives and dies by cash flow. Working capital is like electricity—if there's an outage, everything stops—and ever since that delusional early morning in Asolo, I have kept a firm grip on our financials. This discipline has earned us a high level of credibility with our financial lenders, which has been essential to our success.

What people want to know before doing business with you is simple—are you responsible, and are you reliable? When we share our projections with lenders, they know they can take them to the bank.

The tools and disciplines I put into place that morning remain in place today. As a corporate executive, I listened to too many blissfully optimistic business forecasts. The top leaders constantly praised lower-level managers for their optimistic projections, which kept them from clearly thinking about the more likely outcomes. Then, when their real-life results fell short, they wasted energy explaining why the shortfall wasn't their fault instead of trying to understand why their forecast was so off.

My approach was the opposite. I never pretended to have a crystal ball. I believed in under-promising and over-delivering. I would present the pessimistic side of a plan. When pressed by management, I would explain my logic and discuss the upside *if* everything went perfectly. I would never commit to anything beyond my control or try to persuade myself that something had to happen because I needed it to.

After some tough talk, my boss would accept my forecast and lock it in as part of his own projection. Later, when I sat before the CEO to review my performance vs. forecast, I was usually an over-performer. My peers made their monthly excuses while I was praised for delivering reliably.

Since founding StoreBound, I've gotten to know my bankers as friends. I hear plenty of horror stories about entrepreneurial CEOs over-promising and under-delivering, which inevitably causes difficulties for the bank and shakes their confidence.

As we've grown, our appetite for working capital has become voracious. We often operate outside our borrowing formula and sail through our credit limit, but it's never a surprise to our lender. Months before we have a need beyond our credit facility, I discuss it with the bank. I show them why and to what extent we require the additional capital. I project how long we need to be outside our borrowing formula and when the excess will be repaid. I present my numbers and the facts in the same clear, concise manner I've used in the corporate world for years. I give my full attention to their questions and concerns and address them without heading off into the wild blue yonder of an entrepreneurial-visionary spiel. Magic thinking doesn't help anyone. My under-sell & over-deliver approach resonates much better.

In the early stages of the relationship, our lender put me through the wringer every time I came with a request. Bankers are careful with money—would you want to work with a banker who isn't? They would sit me in a conference room, outnumber me with suits, look at me suspiciously, and then pepper me with questions. I took the time to view my requests from their vantage point before the meeting, which allowed me to anticipate their questions and prepare satisfying answers.

After our fifth meeting, Charles Sharf, the Managing Director of White Oak Commercial Finance, turned to the other people at the table and said, "We need to find more clients like StoreBound who actually have a handle on their business."

Then he looked at me and said, "Evan, whenever you provide us with a projection, you beat it. Every time you commit to paying us back by a certain date, you do it sooner. Do you realize how many of our clients do this?"

"How many clients do you have?"

"Several hundred."

I made a guess. "Half?"

"Only you. You are *it*."

He went on to describe the clients who consistently fail to meet their commitments, then arrive for meetings armed with explanations about their outdated strategies, signaling their intention to pivot.

To me, the concept of pivoting was a last resort. My pragmatic approach was to temper expectations—paint the most conservative view of reality. Then, as things got better or worse, make the small corrections necessary in real time to sidestep the need for disruptive pivots or lengthy excuses.

Winning trust by under-promising and then overdelivering enabled me to grow our business with the confidence of our lender. I knew the bank had my back because I never surprised them. Banks hate surprises; most people in commerce do. Business is not like your birthday. Surprises are not fun—they often signal turbulence, and most of the time, bad news.

This mindset helped me eliminate almost all surprises. It built in a cushion for things that would inevitably go wrong. This made my results predictable, an attribute seldom seen among entrepreneurs. The predictability eventually helped me secure a $40 million line of credit—without giving up a single share of equity in the business.

Of all the things you can control in business, expectations are the easiest. I only share projections that acknowledge the inherent unpredictability of the marketplace and I use robust analytical tools to vigilantly monitor our performance. When changes occur, as they always do, I prioritize timely and transparent communication, reinforcing my commitment to accountability.

Takeaways
CHOOSE DISCIPLINE OVER DISARRAY

- **Know the numbers.**
  Don't wait to get a grip on your numbers—schedule time to keep your figures fresh. Stale numbers are useless. If you're not up to date, you can't make the best decisions. When you keep your financials fresh, you can focus on growing the business and spend your time making an impact.

- **Predictable = trustworthy.**
  When it comes to financials, surprises corrode relationships. If I persuade my banker to take on risk based on unrealistic projections, he will make the same far-fetched commitment to his credit team to get my request approved. If my numbers don't come in as planned, or if I'm not able to pay him back when I said I would, he has to have the same awkward conversation on his side. Inevitably, when he passes along my excuse, it'll sound flimsy, and we both will have lost credibility.

- **Pay attention and you won't have to pivot.**
  The world is dynamic, and the business landscape is constantly changing. Reacting to change is a huge part of leading a company. Instead of resisting change, I allow myself to move with the current.

Bruce Lee's famous "Be like water" quote suggests that we adapt to our environments by changing with them rather than living rigidly. *"If you put water into a cup, it becomes the cup. You put water into a bottle, and it becomes the bottle. Be water, my friend."*

When organizations fail to remain fluid, they are often forced to pivot. Most of the time, a "pivot" is just a positive way of describing a necessary change that happened too late because someone wasn't paying attention to the changes around them. I'd rather make minor corrections along the way so a pivot isn't required to avert disaster. Every day is an opportunity to make minor adjustments, which requires a heightened awareness. Keep your antenna up. The cues are everywhere.

Don't try to fight the current of a powerful river. Be the water and go with it. Use it to your advantage.

17. You Are the Brand

By our third year, things were going well. We had sold millions of dollars to key national retailers. We were still quite far from profitability, but we were fully operational and growing.

It was time to focus on developing a brand to carry us forward to build our legacy. My industry friends suggested licensing a brand, but that didn't sit well with me. Sure, licensing an established brand could provide instant credibility with the consumer; however, we would be bound by the terms and conditions of the brand owner. We'd likely face restrictions around product design, marketing, and distribution channels. I was determined to create our own. It was essential to build value for StoreBound—not the owner of another brand. We would build our brand on a new approach reflecting *our* values. It would allow us to remain in control of our future rather than requiring routine approvals from a Licensor.

New brands were constantly coming and going in categories like pots and pans, gadgets, and mixing bowls. The typical retailer carries hundreds of these brands.

Small appliances were a different story. The brands my parents registered for when they married over 50 years ago still dominated the category. Sunbeam, Hamilton Beach, Oster, Mr. Coffee, Black & Decker, Cuisinart, Crock Pot, and KitchenAid had all withstood the test of time and ruled the retail shelves.

In the earliest stage of launching a start-up, many things that sound easy are anything but. Rachel and I quickly learned how difficult it was to create a strong brand concept that resonated.

For starters, we struggled with a brand name. We wanted something short and succinct, preferably one word. It also needed a website URL close to the name. Over several days, we brainstormed with our creative team, but whenever we came up with something we liked, someone else owned the trademark.

Early in the process, one of our designers said, "What about using your last name—Dash?"

We quickly shut that idea down. We did not want to have the brand associated with us as individuals. Brainstorming continued for over a month. We made tremendous progress on brand attributes and developed a creative look we loved. But our brand-new baby still needed a name.

Rachel and I were scheduled for a grueling two-week trip to China. Before we left, we gave it one last-ditch effort. We wanted to leave the creative team with a brand name to work with while we were away.

Once again, someone floated the idea of using Dash as the name. This time, they tried to sell us based on its connotation with the kitchen.

"You know, a dash of this, a dash of that," the designer said. "It's cute, it's clear, it's a name that immediately belongs in the kitchen."

It was the fifth or sixth time the idea had come up. The team loved the Dash name. Rachel and I still weren't sold.

The morning we returned from China, everyone was in the office, waiting eagerly for us. Our lead designer announced that the team had nailed the name and wanted to present it to us.

They started to play a video they had created with stop-motion animation.

"A Dash of Color."

"A Dash of Flavor."

"Healthy Food in a Dash."

Seeing the name come to life made the brand resonate. The look and feel were everything we wanted.

"Dash just works!" our lead designer suggested. "It's who we are. Quick, young, friendly, adventurous, and fun. Willing to try new flavors—a dash of this, a dash of that. And before you shut us down, guys, try to think of it as a pure coincidence that the brand is also your last name. Subtract yourselves."

We looked through the rest of the creative materials. Everything was brilliant. We loved the logo. The packaging concepts would be the strongest our industry had seen. The marketing concepts were terrific. Rachel and I were smiling the whole time as we reviewed the materials. It was fun, fresh, and playful.

Dash was it.

And so, in 2012, the most dynamic young brand in our industry was born. After months of preparation and a seemingly endless stream of expenses, we arrived at the International Housewares Show for the first public unveiling of Dash. It was March in Chicago, and the trade show floor was quiet and cold when Rachel and I arrived at the crack of dawn. The show wouldn't open to the public for a few hours, but the nervous anticipation drew us to our booth well before we could do anything useful. The samples and graphics were set, our catalogs had arrived, and everything looked great.

We paced. We sat. We paced some more. We took it all in, and we thought it looked fabulous. But it didn't matter what we thought. We were dying to hear the first authentic reactions to what we hoped would be our future. The anticipation created a whirlwind of emotions and nervous energy.

The show's opening represented a pivotal moment, both personally and professionally. It culminated almost two years of hard work, dedication, and investment. Our booth was the first tangible manifestation of our vision and effort, now open for scrutiny. We would finally see Dash through others' eyes, and within 72 hours, we would know if our company stood a chance of making it.

As soon as the show floor opened, it was clear we'd made the right decision for our brand. Hundreds of strangers came into our booth and lit up when they saw our branding. We kept overhearing comments like "I love this!" and "It's so fun!"

Trade shows are a dizzying whirlwind of activity. Exhibitors are easily swept away by the sheer volume of interactions and the endless stream of enthusiastic faces. It's invigorating, but the environment can be deceptive, luring entrepreneurs toward a false sense of achievement. It's a common trap: mistaking the fervor and foot traffic for tangible success.

This might have been our first time as exhibitors, but Rachel and I knew how to measure success. We concentrated on discerning meaningful connections from fleeting interactions. The quantity of enthusiastic reactions to our brand built our confidence, but our focus was on the quality and relevance of our engagements.

Despite drawing over 50,000 attendees, only a handful of individuals held the keys to our success: the decision-makers, the influencers, and the gatekeepers of vast networks—all needles in a haystack of passersby. The challenge and opportunity lay in identifying and connecting with these pivotal few.

In the opening hours, the overwhelming anxiety that had consumed me for months melted away. As my confidence grew, I began searching for that one major customer with the potential to catapult us into the mainstream of American retail. As I gazed down the busy aisles of the show, one face stood out from the crowd. She took in our booth from about a hundred feet away, and her face lit up.

As she walked toward our display, I made eye contact with the friendliest face at the show. She was tall, beautiful, and impeccably dressed—far more stylish than the typical Housewares Show attendee. Her long blond hair bounced with each step, and her smile widened as she approached.

I felt like we knew each other, but I couldn't place how. It was like seeing a celebrity and feeling a sense of familiarity, even though you've never met. It only took a moment for me to figure it out. It was Mindy Grossman, a celebrity in the retail world and the CEO of Home Shopping Network. I had seen her in the recent Forbes list of the Most Powerful Women in the World. And she was making a beeline right toward me.

"This is amazing," she said as she crossed into our booth.

"Thank you so much," I replied with an ear-to-ear grin. "I'm Evan Dash, and this is my wife, Rachel. Let us show you around."

We walked Mindy through the booth, sharing our retail backgrounds and why we launched the company. We connected like old friends, and with each new product, Mindy's enthusiasm grew more contagious.

"I love it! Dash has a story to tell," Mindy began, her voice mixed with excitement and certainty. "HSN is the perfect platform to bring your story to life."

During our brief encounter, Mindy envisioned our range of products on the HSN set, exciting her viewers and eventually transforming mundane cooking routines in millions of homes.

Her insistence on launching Dash nationally was more than a business proposition—it was a testament to her vision and commitment to bringing excitement to her audience.

"I'll have my people stop by to work out the details."

As Mindy left the booth, Rachel and I looked at each other silently. It was clear we could both feel our lives changing. Mindy's instincts were spot on, and within a few years, Dash would become a name buyers were clamoring to have in their stores, and consumers loved using in their kitchens.

With the show's success behind us, we officially locked in the brand and felt inspired to live up to it. Dash implied youthful, fresh, fun, and helpful—everything we wanted to be. Names can be magical. They have an energy. It's not just about marketing; it's also about inspiring the team behind the name. A commitment to Dash was now part of their identity and demanded a set of positive values they could identify with.

With our baby finally named, the real work began. We knew this wasn't a sprint—it was a marathon, and we had to play the long game. Like the fire department, we aimed to build a legacy rooted in doing right by those we served, treating people how *they* wanted to be treated. Our fresh approach demanded fresh tactics. With the priority to create long-term sustainable success driven by resilience, innovation, and trust rather than grasping for instant gains, I turned to a lesson I learned early in life from my mother.

When I was growing up, my mom was a real estate agent. It was long before the internet. Personal relationships were everything. I watched her build a successful career through empathy, patience, and an unrelenting advocacy for her clients.

Her selling tactics were unconventional. Instead of encouraging clients to stretch themselves and their finances to buy a house as soon as possible, I often heard her steer clients away from making a purchase that didn't meet their needs.

In her line of work, if you didn't sell, you didn't earn. Like any commissioned sales job, most people succumb to the temptation of short-term thinking. Close the deal— get paid! But my mom was playing the long game—not because of a grand vision of the future—it's just who she is. Kind, compassionate, empathetic. Her approach was all about building trust. People who bought homes from her—and the people she talked out of buying houses—all had this in common: They quickly learned to trust my mom. And that meant a steady stream of repeat business and referrals.

My mother turned buying and selling real estate into a positive experience for all the participants. Everyone involved in the deal felt she had done right by them. And she had.

I often thought of my mom's approach when starting my own company. She was a very effective salesperson who succeeded by putting her customers' needs above her own. Doing right by her clients inspired them—and the ever-expanding circles of their friends, family members, business associates, and coworkers—to come back over and over.

Customer advocacy was the antithesis of how salespeople were encouraged to operate—one of the reasons I was grateful to have moved on from retail. The strategy was to get the customer to spend as much as possible and do it quickly. And if it wasn't what the customer needed or even really wanted, well, they could shoot for something better next time.

Most salespeople I've encountered use some form of high-pressure tactics. I'm more comfortable with education and advocacy. It worked for my mom as I watched her build a resilient and self-generating business that endured for decades.

Advocating for the customer's best interests changes how a salesperson sees themself. Clients aren't just potential transactions; they are people with unique needs and desires. A salesperson pushes products, whereas an advocate supports people. By taking the time to understand their needs, my mom put families into homes that were perfect for them. Even if it took longer, their satisfaction ensured their loyalty.

The advocacy approach requires patience, something most salespeople don't exactly teem with. But patience improves your odds of satisfying the client with a deal that feels right for everyone, and very likely, repeat business and a string of referrals will be the reward.

Trust is hard to earn, easy to lose, and nearly impossible to regain. My mom understood that her reputation hinged on the trust she built with her clients, the same way I understood the credibility dynamic with my bank lender. Whenever she advised clients against a purchase that was not a good fit for them, she demonstrated that she cared more about their family's well-being than her commission. Her approach cemented long-term relationships with her clients.

When I founded StoreBound, exercising patience was the hardest part. Initially, we were hemorrhaging money while revenue was still a trickle. It was scary, but my mom's example gave me the courage to trust the long-term approach. The art of selling is not a short-term game of numbers. It's a long road of investing in relationships, building trust, and striving for mutual satisfaction.

There's a distinguishable line between building a brand and crafting a legacy. It's akin to the difference between a house and a home. One is a structure, whereas the other is steeped in emotion, memories, and a sense of belonging. Our vision was never about marking our presence—rather, it was about being remembered. We aspired to craft a legacy—our brand was merely the foundation. I knew it would take much more than superior products or savvy marketing. It required a steadfast commitment to our customers—genuine partnerships over transactions, which became the ethos of our selling tactics. Our goal wasn't making a sale—it was forging trust, loyalty, and an emotional bond.

Today, our philosophy of doing right by customers is encapsulated in our mission of 'Winning Hearts.' It's more than a strategy; it's the core of who we are. And it ensures that customers don't just purchase our products; they champion our brand and amplify our story.

Takeaways

YOU ARE THE BRAND

- **Put yourself into your brand.**
  Not your name necessarily, but certainly your values. While navigating the first formative years, it's easy for a company's direction to waver. A strong brand serves as a beacon, keeping the team laser-focused on the mission even as they encounter the unpredictable waves of the market. When employees recognize the brand's ethos, they become ambassadors and uphold its principles, and customers who identify with what your brand stands for are likely yours to keep.

- **Leaders make things happen.**
  When Mindy Grossman left our booth, a new partnership was already brewing and would soon unfold into a success story. HSN quickly became our first national customer and preferred launch partner for new products. Our success with HSN showcased the power of discerning leadership and the magic of finding the right offering at the right time. For Mindy and HSN, Dash was not just another brand; it was a gateway to redefining the home cooking experience for their audience.

- **Reorders are a great measure of success.**
  Shortly after launching our brand, a national department store buyer asked to buy our Chef Series Blender, a best-selling item on Home Shopping Network. When I declined, her astonishment was evident.

"You're a brand-new company, and you're turning down my order," the buyer protested.

"I don't care about orders. I care about *re-orders*. Our blender needs to be demonstrated, or it won't sell. You can't run these demos, so I'd rather forgo the business than create a problem for you."

Two years later, after we had built a multi-million-dollar business together, she confided, "Your honesty the first time we met made me commit. No one had ever prioritized my needs over a sale. That's when I realized I could trust you 100%, and I was all in."

I had forgotten all about the blender situation. The buyer certainly hadn't.

- **Building a legacy is a marathon, not a sprint.** Every brand etched into the fabric of our daily lives began as someone's crazy idea. It's easy to forget that even the most-loved brands were unfamiliar once and had to fight for their place in the market.

  We recognized that trust and reputation are earned—built brick by brick with quality products, great experiences, and a strong, unique voice—repeated over and over and over. We were looking at years—maybe decades—of commitment, persistence, and resilience to etch our brand into the collective consciousness of consumers. The stakes were high. Dash was, after all, our name. The goal wasn't just to launch a branded product line. From the start, we aimed to build a legacy.

18. Write a Survival Story

On May 31, 1999, the headline *Amazon Dot Bomb* ran on the cover of Barron's, the highly regarded financial publication. The article's intro read, *"The idea that Amazon CEO Jeff Bezos has pioneered a new business paradigm is silly. He's just another middleman, and the stock market is beginning to catch on to that fact."* By 2001, Amazon's stock dropped below $10 per share, more than 90% below its previous highs.

And we all know how that turned out.

In 2018, when an employee inquired about Amazon's future at an all-hands meeting in Seattle, Bezos replied, "I predict one day Amazon will fail. Amazon will go bankrupt."

Bezos explained that the lifespans of large companies are typically 30-plus years, not 100-plus years. He emphasized the key to prolonging Amazon's longevity was to "obsess over customers." The first two decades of Amazon's continuity are directly attributable to Jeff Bezos doing everything necessary to ensure its survival.

Since my first day as an entrepreneur, I had one haunting obsession: survival. That crystallized during my panic episode in Italy when I thought everything had come crashing down. Even with the best tools and discipline in place, the fire department taught me how swiftly a stable situation can unravel. Wrecks and disasters happen every day, generally because no one expects them. Knowing that I would have to steer the company through inevitable periods of uncertainty was a weight that always loomed. Fortunately, it didn't seem like we'd face serious challenges any time soon.

We had cemented our reputation as problem solvers, and orders flowed in daily from our buyers. We had surpassed all early expectations and were celebrating achieving $10 million in annual sales. Things couldn't be going better.

And that's when it often happens, right? Danger lurking around the corner, waiting to crush everything you've worked so hard to build.

It often starts with a phone call from a lawyer. Like a bolt of lightning out of a clear, blue sky, a lawsuit threatened to wipe us out. A prominent competitor accused us of infringing on one of their patents. They were seeking over $1 million in damages. Losing the case would bankrupt us.

I was in shock. We followed procedures to ensure we didn't violate anyone else's intellectual property. In my retail days, I had distanced myself from companies that copied innovative suppliers. I respected genuine creation and shunned anything that reeked of imitation.

As I read through the lawsuit, a whirlwind of emotions engulfed me. Initially, it was like a sharp, disorienting jolt —like plunging into icy water. That quickly transformed into confusion, my mind racing to piece together how such a claim could even arise. By the time I finished reading, a simmering frustration set in—a mix of indignation and disbelief. But beneath these layers was a nagging anxiety. The shadow of uncertainty and what it meant to the future of my business would accompany me day and night for the foreseeable future.

I sought counsel from Brian Belles, our business-minded patent attorney, who had written a Freedom-to-Operate letter, an opinion that was supposed to shield us from infringement allegations. The reality, however, was that patent cases can be subjective and unpredictable. Brian was confident in our position, but we couldn't stop the competitor from seeking damages. Infringement or not, the path forward looked like a long and expensive fight.

The courtroom would be a risky battleground to defend the virtue of our position. Despite my lawyer's confidence, a judge or jury could see it differently, and one rap of the gavel could seal our fate. The thought of ceding control of our future to an indifferent third party was unbearable.

Brian referred me to a trial lawyer he described as "an effective and practical litigator," meaning a sole practitioner we might be able to afford. The litigator and I convened the next day in my office. After examining the patent and products, he said he was confident we hadn't infringed.

Before I could get excited, he cautioned that we were still looking at a grim picture: the immense resources of our adversary, a court known to favor patent holders, and a giant legal firm ready to pounce. They could overwhelm us with demands or bankrupt us with legal fees before we ever made it into court.

I couldn't afford the expense, much less the mental toll of a prolonged lawsuit. Despite the product's significance to our business, I was willing to walk away from it, concede fault, and negotiate a fair settlement. Anything seemed better than facing litigation.

Determined to get out alive, I called the Plaintiff's president directly. Our conversation was cordial, and I proposed several concessions if they dismissed the suit, but he remained unmoved. He wouldn't even discuss a path forward before referring me to his legal counsel for any future communication. I hung up discouraged. Diplomacy, usually my strength, had failed me.

Weeks turned into months. The passing time was a punishing test of my resolve. The attorneys made little progress; no matter what we tried, they refused to drop or settle the case. My faith in the justice system wavered as I watched our business lose traction. I was personally consumed. We lost momentum. I started to doubt whether I could ensure StoreBound's survival. Feeling helpless, I decided to take matters into my own hands one more time.

When I made another call to their president, he wasn't happy to hear from me but reluctantly agreed to hear me out. By the end of our call, he gave me a glimmer of hope when he said, "You seem sincere, and you have a great reputation. I'm willing to meet face-to-face to see if we can put this behind us."

We set a meeting for that Saturday in California. I booked a flight and reserved a conference room at an airport hotel. I brought everything I could possibly need to work toward a resolution—the products, our marketing materials, all my engineering documents and schematics, and everything else related to our business. I wanted to be ready for anything.

He arrived empty-handed but right on time. We shook hands and sat across the table, where he immediately clarified their firm stance. Since we didn't know each other, I delved deep into my career journey, emphasizing the integrity I brought to each position. I assured him that I didn't start my company to be a pirate or a copycat, then showed marketing materials with our new innovations. I aimed to reassure him of my genuine intentions.

The room was thick with tension, and despite the emotional toll, I maintained a humble and sincere demeanor. He was polite and professional but retained a resolute front throughout. I held my breath when he scribbled something on an index card, hoping it indicated progress.

Remarkably, within an hour, we reached a tentative agreement. He told me he respected my approach and could see why his colleagues held me in high regard. When he made the call to instruct his attorneys to wrap up the matter, it felt like dawn breaking after the longest, darkest night.

I was so energized on the flight home. My attention could finally refocus on the horizon of possibilities. The ordeal had instilled a profound awareness of the perils of our legal system and provided some new strategies for my playbook.

Takeaways
WRITE A SURVIVAL STORY

- **Eyes on the prize.**
  Even when you're right, litigation can be costly, draining, and potentially catastrophic. My attorney's conviction in my case was secondary; my primary concern was survival. Conflict is a massive distraction, and the looming threat of a devastating legal outcome and the overwhelming fees were too great a gamble. When survival is at stake, sometimes the wisest move is to concede, offer a sincere apology, shoulder the losses, and move on. Accepting a momentary setback allowed us to stay in the game.

  Unfortunately, legal battles seem like a rite of passage on the road to building a resilient business. Years ago, my corporate litigator, Richard Kaye, shared two pieces of invaluable advice that have guided me on both sides of a lawsuit:

  1. Courts are not arenas for justice. They are a place for decisions.

  2. Sometimes, it's better to walk away without a fight because living well is the best revenge.

  While not advantageous to his billings, he encouraged me to defuse conflicts swiftly and refocus on success.

- **It doesn't always have to be Game of Thrones.** Negotiation experts might have advised starting from a position of strength. Perhaps filing a countersuit and pretending I had the wherewithal for a drawn-out battle. Make them blink first, so *they* back down.

  But what if they called my bluff? I wasn't ready to poke the bear to see how it reacted. If things escalated, there might be no going back. Instead, I chose to appeal to their sense of humanity. I couldn't imagine their president executing a humble businessman who posed no threat. This wasn't *Game of Thrones,* so I played the game with my cards face up. I revealed our vulnerability and conceded the battle, which allowed him to provide the outcome we both needed.

19. If You Don't Learn from Failure, You're Just Failing

By 2016, we achieved over $25 million in annual sales. The Dash brand was driving our growth, and retailers were knocking on our door to carry the line. With a winning concept on our hands, we focused on developing enough products to make a strong statement on the selling floor. We poured our efforts into new product development and began the tradition of celebrating our failures.

We take pride in pushing boundaries. When we're successful, we celebrate. Our stumbles? They, too, deserve a round of applause. Because if we're not stumbling occasionally, are we even moving forward?

Developing a new product is always risky. In the traditional approach, a creative team kicks off a series of brainstorming sessions. To stay grounded, they perform some degree of research on the marketplace. However, the development process is often flawed from the get-go. A group of like-minded individuals, products of the same corporate cultures brainstorming, can inadvertently become an echo chamber.

Once the team settles on their great new-product concept, they dive into designing, prototyping, and refining their thingamajig, then get ready to introduce it to retailers. Each stage can take weeks, months, or even years and consume tremendous financial and human resources.

Finally, the most refined prototypes are carried like precious trophies to a trade show and shown to select potential customers in a back room, away from the eyes of the public. These key customers are expected to provide helpful feedback, and maybe they will. But tradeshow feedback is often unreliable, even dangerous. Everyone is in an upbeat mood and focused on innovating the future, and often, the concepts that dazzle at a trade show miss making the crucial connection with actual, real, live consumers.

Assuming a positive trade show response, the real work and considerable investments begin. Going from art to part is expensive and risky. After absorbing the customer feedback and one last round of refinements, a manufacturer is contracted to make the idea into a product ready to be commercialized. With the market trending toward smart devices, development might also require an additional layer of hardware and software development, as well as circuit board design, the incorporation of Bluetooth and Wi-Fi modules, coding apps for both iOS and Android, cloud service connections, security protocols, and of course, debugging to make sure all the elements connect and perform as expected.

Finally, giant molds are fabricated to mass-produce the parts for assembly. For a typical electrical product, like the ones we sell, the upfront investment can easily run between $500,000 and $1 million before any inventory is purchased. And depending on the response from the market and the retailers' appetite, the inventory investment could run into the millions.

All this capital is being spent before the new product generates dollar one of revenue. It's a leap of faith with no safety net.

Now for the sobering truth: Most consumer product launches are flops, failing to resonate with their audience. The result is expensive dust collectors on retail shelves. And the retailers have return privileges to send unsold products back to the supplier, which they take full advantage of. That can bankrupt a small company. Game over.

Still, most entrepreneurs throw caution to the wind when launching a product. It's the 'Leap of Faith' model. Occasionally, it works. Mostly, it doesn't.

With our dream on the line, I wasn't willing to take blind leaps. We needed a way to gauge consumer interest in innovative products without the risk of overwhelming losses. The answer to this dilemma came at the dawn of crowdfunding—not to be confused with crowdsourcing.

On crowd*sourcing* sites like Quirky, a user posts a new product design, which then gets refined by a collective of other creatives who, driven by potential earnings, enhance the original idea.

Crowd*funding*, on the other hand, allows anyone with a product idea to pre-sell their concept and raise funds to commercialize the idea. If site users like a project, they can play venture capitalist, backing a project they believe in. It's a win-win. Creatives get instant feedback and much-needed capital, and contributors become early adopters, getting the product before the public.

Crowdfunding allowed our start-up to push the innovation envelope with a high degree of risk management. Emerging platforms like Kickstarter and Indiegogo acted like crystal balls, allowing us to post new concepts and gain feedback from a large audience of potential consumers. Gone were the days of relying on the whims of a few retail "insiders" to predict the market's appetite. Instead, crowdfunding allowed us to lay our cards on the table for actual consumers. Their monetary support became our yardstick. If a concept struck a chord, the pre-orders rolled in, offering the assurance we craved to greenlight further investment.

In the years following our launch, we successfully funded five different innovations using crowdfunding campaigns, raising almost $5 million before the products were even made. It was focus group perfection—strangers voting with their hard-earned dollars. However, even more useful than the successful campaigns were the ones that didn't take flight. Our real-time market validation was just as effective at revealing the losers, sparing us the immense losses of bringing them to market.

Take, for example, The Health Cube, our vision of a blender for the future. As conceived, it would have been the first Wi-Fi-enabled "Smart Blender" with recipes created by top chefs and powered by a computer to produce perfect results every time. I was obsessed with the idea.

First, some backstory. About a year after we launched Dash with a juicer and egg cooker, we followed it with the Dash Chef Series Digital Blender. That blender is a beast! It has a two-horsepower motor, six Japanese surgical steel blades, and six pre-programmed functions to make anything from ice cream or the perfect smoothie all the way to gluten-free flour or piping hot soup. We launched it on the Home Shopping Network in 2013. Instant success. It became our best-selling product, with top customer ratings.

Many retail customers suggested we take it to the next level and make a connected version. It would enable unlimited blending programs and an entire library of recipes that the user could update online. IoT (Internet of Things) devices were gaining popularity, so we figured the timing was perfect to take our blender into the cloud.

We built a development plan and dubbed our wonder child the *Health Cube,* or H3. We estimated it would cost almost $1 million to develop the hardware and software for the H3 and then fabricate the tooling necessary to mass-produce the parts. The manufactured unit cost would be nearly double the current model because of the sophisticated electronics necessary to connect the blender to the internet.

The project would require an enormous investment—the mobile app alone would cost us over $200,000 to develop—and there was no precedent to suggest if something like this would be widely accepted by the consumer.

We loved the concept and believed the consumer would too, but before we committed to the investment, we turned to crowdfunding to validate whether there was a market. We created a beautiful campaign, *The Health Cube: Your Kitchen's First Robot,* and launched it on Kickstarter. We already had a large Instagram following, so we were able to market the campaign to the right audience. We sent our messaging to a quarter-million consumers who loved our brand and were interested in a healthy lifestyle. We expected nothing less than a screaming success.

Well, not this time. We launched the campaign to the sound of silence. Someone even checked to make sure our internet was online. In the first five days of the campaign, only four backers pre-ordered the H3—three of whom worked in our company.

In almost every other business situation I've been in, everyone at this point would be pointing fingers at what didn't work and whose fault it was. However, Rachel and I were cultivating a company culture that encouraged intellectual honesty and self-awareness. We weren't interested in blaming. *Coulda, woulda, shoulda*—forget that. We were proud of our team's execution of the project. Okay, the consumer just wasn't ready for such an advanced product. Maybe they would never want this level of sophistication in an ordinary product like a blender. Regardless, it was time to celebrate. We'd dodged a major bullet. Without crowdfunding, we would have kept pushing development forward and wasted our money and time. It could have become a catastrophic mistake and taken our company down.

Instead, we were able to immediately refocus our attention on something completely different—a simple, inexpensive product that would be intuitive, fun to use, and work flawlessly. Later that year, we launched our Mini Makers—adorable little griddles and waffle makers. We designed them with a cute and friendly appearance and manufactured them in a variety of fresh colors not typically found in kitchen appliances. The Mini Makers have become one of the best-selling products in our industry. We've sold well over 30 million units.

Our Mini Makers became a transformative product for our company and allowed us to win the hearts of millions and millions of consumers. The goodwill we have created by putting these little beauties into millions of kitchens was better than any marketing campaign we could have run. These products are a perfect entry point for consumers to experience the Dash brand, and they sprung out of a failure to become the foundation of our business.

Failure doesn't have to equal disaster. Failure can be a useful waypoint on the road to success, especially if you're careful about mitigating risk.

Takeaways

IF YOU DON'T LEARN FROM FAILURE, YOU'RE JUST FAILING

- **Nothing succeeds like failure.**
  Thomas Edison said, "I have not failed. I've just found 10,000 ways that won't work." Embracing failure is not just about resilience; it's a fundamental part of innovation. It's about being willing to try new things and take risks, understanding that failure is a likely outcome and often necessary for breakthroughs.

  Failure forces us to rethink, question, innovate, and push the boundaries of what is possible. Failing challenges our assumptions and requires us to approach problems from different perspectives. Failure can be disappointing and painful, but it is a crucible for growth and learning.

- **Sometimes, less is more.**
  Our ambitious IoT Blender, though promising on paper, didn't make the anticipated splash. In our quest for technological sophistication and performance, we overlooked a fundamental truth: Consumers often yearn for simplicity coupled with a dash of fun. It wasn't cutting-edge tech they craved but rather a product that blended ease with enjoyment. Without the failure of the IoT Blender, we would have never launched our Mini Makers—our most successful product to date. Our experimentation and adaptability provided a constant source of fuel for our business.

20. Partnerships & Multipliers

We were a small, dynamic company, built on a sturdy foundation and poised to accelerate our growth. Recognizing strength in numbers inclined me to seek smart alliances and unique collaborations that would yield positive results beyond what each party could achieve independently.

I first experienced the power of brand collaborations in the 1990s when the premier cookware brand, All-Clad, teamed up with the well-known and beloved culinary personality, Julia Child, to launch the *Julia Pan by All-Clad*. With a unique pan, a perfectly shaped spoon, and a book of recipes from Julia's archive, it was the perfect gift for any culinary enthusiast. The combination of the two brands was an instant success.

The housewares industry has been no stranger to celebrity endorsements. Still, there was something about the Julia Pan that perfectly blended the DNA of All-Clad with America's most beloved kitchen personality. It was the perfect marriage between a world-class manufacturer and the person who could get that piece of equipment to do amazing things.

I had only seen this type of partnership in Formula One racing, where a machine is paired with a driver, and they perform as one. Think Michael Schumacher and Ferrari. Together, they posted 72 wins, including the World Driver's Championship in 2000, Ferrari's first since 1973.

Since the beginning of the company, I wanted to create the same magic. When we launched, big brand collaborations were becoming all the rage. Some seemed perfectly paired, while others were almost shocking, like Pepsi x Peeps. Some felt natural, like Gucci x Fiat—two iconic Italian brands. Fiat built the car, but Gucci made it bespoke, adding their branded interlocking G's leather to adorn the interior. The signature Gucci green and red stripes on the outside of the car made it Fiat's most desirable and newsworthy product launch ever.

Introducing our own brand, Dash, was the most daunting but liberating experience I have ever had in business. On the one hand, we lacked the instant credibility and trust that consumers bestowed on our iconic competitors like Cuisinart or KitchenAid. On the other hand, if we could get Dash to resonate with the American consumer, we would have something extraordinarily valuable that we made from scratch.

The hallmarks of our brand were aimed at younger consumers. We looked fun, fresh, colorful, approachable—and most importantly, unknown. Being unknown turned out to be an asset. Being *unknown* meant we could be *discovered.*

When we launched the Dash brand in 2012, Instagram was our most important marketing tool. It was all we could afford. Facebook had not yet acquired Instagram and imposed their plans to monetize the platform. We couldn't even pay to advertise or "up-level" our posts to get more visibility. The only way to get eyeballs was to create content people liked, engaged with, and shared. When overall engagement with a post hit a certain level, that post was featured on the "popular page"—the original Instagram landing page seen by everyone opening the app. In one week, three of our posts made it onto the popular page, each time landing us over 10,000 new followers.

Within six months, we had more followers than the largest brands in our industry. People started to take notice—especially retail buyers.

Fortunately, our competitors failed to realize our angle was 180° different from theirs.

The big brands couldn't resist pounding their chests whenever they posted. "Look at us! Look at this new product! Look at our chef! Look at us at the food and wine festival! Look at me! Buy me! Me! Me! Me!"

And they came off like an obnoxious dinner guest. The guy who dominates the conversation, bragging about what he does and what he has, showing zero interest in the people around him. The guy who never gets invited back.

We, on the other hand, were the unknown, young, attractive dinner guest who surprises with a wonderful personality. We were interested in everyone around us. We listened. We told interesting stories—we were all about *engaging*. And by the end of the night, everyone at the party was following us on social media. They wanted to know what we were up to. They wanted to stay in touch.

Rather than making our social media all about us, we made it about our audience. We posted healthy recipes and taught simple cooking techniques. We inspired people to make healthy meals at home. We were colorful and fun to look at. We were authentic, accessible, energetic, and happy to answer everyone's questions and comments.

Our following continued to outpace the industry. We knew we were on the right track. Thousands of people touched that little blue 'follow' button, signaling they wanted us in their daily social feeds. And we didn't take it for granted.

Within two years, our following had grown to almost one million across multiple accounts, each offering a different style of content. Shortly after crossing the one million mark, we met with a large retailer who was not yet familiar with our brand. After showing our products to the buyer, she pondered for a moment, then said, "I'm not sure your brand will resonate with the consumer."

I grabbed my phone and showed her the size of our social media following. Then I pulled up her company's Instagram, which had less than ten percent of our following. "Respectfully, I'd be more concerned that your brand isn't resonating with the customer."

"Guess I need to update my resume," she said with a smile, and we shared a laugh that diffused what could have been a tense moment.

"Seriously, our following has broken through to a younger customer," I told her. "And we can mobilize this customer to shop in your stores."

She immediately saw my point and allowed us to get started with a test. It turned out to be a great match, and by the end of the second year, we were their fastest-growing brand.

Rather than pushing for sales on social media, we were sharing useful content and gaining followers in return. Our vast audience established our credibility with retailers; we were already a hit with the younger consumers they sought to attract. As our momentum built, we began collaborating with influencers to spark excitement. Together, we launched products, leveraging our combined audiences for greater reach and impact. We've also forged successful co-branded partnerships with brands like Weight Watchers, Delish, and notable personalities in the culinary, fitness, and nutrition arena. We designed these short-term collaborations to generate buzz around one or two product launches.

During our first decade, we only embarked on one long-term partnership, and it has been our most successful—

with Iron Chef Geoffrey Zakarian. The partnership was built on shared values and our admiration for Geoffrey's uncompromising standards and his gift for teaching.

Geoffrey's rise to culinary prominence began at Le Cirque from 1983 to 1987. During these formative years, he staged in the renowned kitchens of Arpège and Au Quai des Ormes in Paris, Aubèrge de l'Ill in Alsace, The Dorchester in London, Le Chantecler with Jacques Maximin in Nice, and Pierre Orsay in Lyon. In 1987, Zakarian took his first turn as Executive Chef at the legendary 21Club in Manhattan. In 1988, he became the Executive Chef of 44 at the Royalton Hotel before opening the Blue Door at the Delano Hotel in Miami in 1995. His culinary prowess continued to shine as he assumed the role of Executive Chef at Patroon in 1997, where he was awarded Three Stars by *The New York Times*.

Geoffrey entered the realm of restaurant ownership in 2001, where his ventures garnered widespread critical acclaim, including a Michelin Star and becoming the first New York chef to earn three consecutive Three Star reviews from *The New York Times*. He was also tapped to conceptualize food and beverage programs for esteemed partners, including The Plaza Hotel, The Water Club at Borgata, and Norwegian Cruise Lines. With a career as diverse as it is illustrious, Geoffrey has risen to prominence as an award-winning cookbook author, a prominent television host, and the Chairman of City Harvest, an organization dedicated to combating hunger in the heart of New York City.

As Geoffrey's portfolio of projects continues to grow, everything that bears the Zakarian name reflects his unwavering commitment to authenticity, design, quality, and his lifelong passion for la belle vie—the good life. Much like Rachel and me, Geoffrey's business endeavors are deeply rooted in a close-knit family circle, with his wife, Margaret, skillfully serving as President of Zakarian Hospitality. Margaret's business acumen and operational expertise seamlessly complement Geoffrey's vision and creativity. As we got to know one another, our friendship blossomed quickly.

Whenever we got together, the conversation inevitably turned toward collaborating to craft professional-grade kitchen tools tailored for home use. Geoffrey, Margaret, Rachel, and I brainstormed product ideas for nearly three years. To get Geoffrey excited about a product, it had to be a game-changer. The goal was to revolutionize the cooking experience at home. Nothing less. One day, while working in Geoffrey's kitchen, it finally happened.

For the better part of two years, Rachel and I had been working with a key manufacturer to apply nonstick coating onto traditional cast-iron cookware. For hundreds of years, the allure of cast iron has been its unparalleled durability, remarkable heat retention, and the fact that it just gets better with age. However, those benefits can be overshadowed by less-than-appealing features. Cast iron cookware is hard to clean. Soap is the enemy—cast iron has to be kept out of the dishwasher and seasoned with oil to prevent rusting. Everyday acidic foods, like tomatoes, can break down the metal.

Our groundbreaking innovation was about to revolutionize an age-old kitchen classic by merging nonstick convenience with cast iron's legacy. The iron rules that had existed for hundreds of years could be tossed out. Plus, cleanup was a breeze—just wipe out the pan, and it's ready to go again.

It was a radically different approach to a product with a cult-like following, so we weren't sure whether Geoffrey and, more importantly, the consumer would accept it. The magic moment occurred when Geoffrey, with the pan blazing hot, seared one of the most delicious steaks I had ever tasted. When I saw his reaction to the pan's performance and then caught his genuine look of amazement when he was able to clean it in a few seconds, I knew we had a game-changer.

This synergy—our groundbreaking innovation and Geoffrey's culinary magic—was worth the wait. The stage was set, and there was only one way to bring such a breakthrough innovation to market—live TV shopping. We would take it to the best of the best—QVC and its audience of over 350 million households in seven countries.

We worked with the QVC team for nearly a year to plan the product's debut. QVC would beam their broadcast straight from our biggest trade show, where Geoffrey would introduce the pans from our booth with a skillful, yet down-to-earth Iron Chef cookfest. QVC's customers at home could buy the pans just as major retailers saw them for the first time.

Pulling off a live TV shopping event from the floor of a tradeshow was a Herculean task. It took an army of people, millions of dollars of equipment, a direct satellite uplink, and, of course, David Venable, America's favorite TV shopping host, to ham it up with our own Geoffrey Zakarian. The instant chemistry between Geoffrey and David was electrifying. It looked like two long-lost friends bonding over something extraordinary that neither one could believe. Six minutes, a few demonstrations, a little tasting, one of David's signature happy dances, and there it was—the "sold out" logo across the screen. Before retailers at the show could register what they were seeing, we had sold thousands of nonstick cast iron pans to QVC's kitchen enthusiasts across America.

Many celebrities casually endorse products, lending their names to make a quick buck. That wasn't in Geoffrey's DNA. His passion for breakthrough kitchen tools was contagious and our partnership was off to the races. Since the initial launch on QVC, we've introduced over 100 SKUs and sold over $50 million of *Zakarian by Dash* products.

Sometime during our first year at QVC, Geoffrey and I went to dinner at a restaurant in Pennsylvania. The reservation was in my name, but he was instantly recognized. The chef sent out some delicious creations from the kitchen before we'd even ordered. As we enjoyed the meal, several fans approached Geoffrey, hoping for a picture or autograph. Every request was met with genuine warmth, and he made each person feel like an old friend as he posed for pictures.

After the fifth time, I asked, "Does this ever bother you?"

He smiled. "Not at all. I'm thankful each time. If no one approached me, that's when I'd have a problem."

And that's the mark of a great partnership—when both sides share common values and are proud to be in business together.

Takeaways

PARTNERSHIPS & MULTIPLIERS

- **Great partnerships should be game-changers.**
  In great partnerships, collaboration doesn't just add value; it multiplies it. The right strategic partner unlocks a force multiplier, propelling each side to a new stratosphere of success that neither could achieve alone.

- **It's not about a first date.**
  Accelerating momentum in business is crucial, especially when the gears are in motion, but rushing into a partnership can be disastrous. The industry saw our collaboration with Geoffrey Zakarian come out of nowhere and become an instant success. But this was not a serendipitous partnership. It was built on a foundation of trust. We had meticulously sculpted it. It was the product of half a decade of engineering, financial modeling, relationship building, and aligned values.

  Patience, common purpose, and shared values significantly improve your chances that this partnership is the right one.

- **Those triple wins.**
  I aim for deals where three parties emerge victorious: the seller, the buyer, and the consumer. A triple-win disrupts the dispiriting notion that business is a zero-sum game. Pursuing win-win-wins steers our company toward sustainable success, but it requires a shift in perspective.

Instead of chasing short-term gains, we obsess over long-term value. Instead of focusing on individual or company success, we aim for collective victories. The triple-win philosophy sets us apart in today's ferocious business landscape. There are no losers when business is rooted in authenticity, purpose, and genuine commitment to value.

21. No Culture, No Company

Our start-up had started and then some. The Dash brand approached $50 million in annual sales in just five years. Our focus on enriching the lives of others continued to supercharge our growth. We had created a virtuous loop and proven the efficacy of our 'winning hearts' approach: offer great products, solve retailer problems, charge a fair price, create great user experiences, amass social media followers and five-star reviews—then watch sales grow. And grow.

We were becoming a formidable business, and Rachel and I decided it was time to double down on the company culture we had nurtured. An authentic and inspired culture would help us continue to thrive in the good years and outperform our competition during tough times.

Since day one, company culture has been on our minds. Rachel and I both had experienced toxic, no-growth company cultures. We dreamed of creating the type of inspired, empowering culture that I experienced in the firehouse and that we both had missed in the corporate world.

Our start-up offered us a blank slate. No legacy systems. No toxic old-timers. No built-in frustrations. No dispiriting rituals. If we failed, only ourselves to blame.

We constantly talked about the environment we wanted to create around us. One day, standing in our kitchen, Rachel said, "We have to make sure we're offering our team a great work-life balance."

"F work-life balance," I replied.

"What? You don't think people deserve—"

"It's the phrase—'work-life balance.' It's a messed-up concept."

Rachel gave me her side eye—that disapproving look when I cross some invisible line she has drawn. It happens a lot.

"Okay," I said, "let me explain. I don't buy into 'work-life balance' because it's *all* life, right? There shouldn't need to be a separation. The idea that you're only living when you leave work—c'mon! That's a horrible existence. Most people spend the most awake, engaged, and inspired hours of their lives at work. So, let's build on that. Let's see work for what it is—a huge part of life. Let's make it a wonderful part of life."

Rachel's smile suggested that we were on the same page after all. Over the following weeks, as we brainstormed business ideas, we started referring to our team of imaginary employees as "our chosen family." We hadn't hired anyone yet, but that was precisely what we planned to do—choose the right people to join our team. And we developed a hierarchy of values that our culture would champion: health first, then family, and then work.

Health comes first, period. It is the foundation upon which almost every aspect of our lives depends. Health has to be everyone's top priority. Good health amplifies our ability to care for our family, excel in our profession, and lead fulfilling lives. Healthy people can give their best when it matters most.

Next, family. Family comes before work. You should be there if your partner or child has a doctor's appointment.

You should be there if there is an event at school during the day. If your kids are involved in activities, go and support them. You should never feel your job is more important than your health or family.

When I played school sports, it meant so much when I scanned the bleachers and saw my parents. I did the same for my kids, and I encourage everyone on my work team to do the same for theirs. In our company, there are no repercussions for missing time at work to care for your health or to demonstrate to your family that they come first.

After health and family comes work. And not just work, as in clocking in the hours while performing your basic job function. We're talking about working as a member of an inspired team with shared values and common goals. Your responsibility is to make us better every day. You must champion our mission, impact our results, and bring out the very best in others on the team. Be a firefighter: Act with purpose, support your teammates, and connect your actions to winning hearts.

When a new prospect comes in for an interview, they are led through our office. The tour takes them winding around all the people working, then back to my office, where we have our discussion. As CEO of a growing company without a clearly defined hierarchy, I'm often asked, "Who would I report to?"

My answer is always the same. "Did you see all those people you walked past on your way to my office? You're accountable to every single one of them. You are accountable to everyone who relies on this company for their livelihood."

If they smile, it's a good early 'tell' that they might be a good fit for our team. An authentic, unrehearsed smile suggests that they appreciate the shocking novelty of being responsible to the team and understand that it implies that everyone would be accountable to them.

My one non-negotiable when hiring is that you must *care*. I'm confident I can teach the right person to do almost any job in the organization, but I can't teach anyone to *care*. People either care or they don't. Without people who genuinely care about their work, we could never maintain a winning-hearts culture.

Going into an interview with the CEO, people anticipate a challenging—even aggressive—session. I don't do that. Instead, I dig to see if they have that caring gene in their DNA.

I start by sizing up whether they care about themselves. What do they take pride in? Do they prioritize their health? What do they do for fun? How do they treat people around them? Where do they live? What condition is their house in? What's been breaking down, and for how long? What type of improvement projects have they done? How do they get along with their neighbors? Do they support charities or volunteer their time?

Their responses suggest how much they care about themselves and their communities.

Next, I want to understand their family life. What sacrifices do they make for those people they love the most? What do they do to protect their families or to enable their success? How and whom do they teach? What doors do they open? What is their relationship like with their significant other? How do they treat the people they love the most?

If they don't go the extra mile for those people, they certainly won't for their coworkers.

Finally, I need to know if they care about their work. What are relationships like with the people they work with? What have they done to make the workplace better? Have they mentored younger team members? How do they deal with conflict at work? Do they accept responsibility for failure? What are they most proud of? How do they feel when customers are let down? What do they do when coworkers disappoint? How do they respond?

This line of questioning can quite accurately ascertain whether the candidate carries that *caring* gene in their DNA. If they do, they'll likely be a good fit for our team.

When you build a team of people who care, chances are your company culture will be inspired, unafraid, and successful—so long as you, the leader, don't screw it up.

When you build a team that cares, no one comes to work in the morning scheming to make someone else's day worse. People are committed to making everyone's day better. Experienced people enjoy training younger team members and empowering them with responsibility. Caring people are consensus-builders, not soulless managers ramming their agendas down other people's throats. They understand that all cross-functional teams must pull together to enable any one individual or group to achieve their goals.

I want to work with people who are passionate about what they do—highly driven self-starters. Waiting around patiently for instructions? Nope, that's not how it works with me. I only work with people who think for themselves and instinctively move toward great results.

People passionate about their work are motivated to excel. Passion drives creativity, sparks innovation, and fuels a thirst for knowledge and improvement. In a company culture that rewards passion, everyone benefits from better performance, increased job satisfaction, and a stimulating work environment.

Creating and sustaining such a culture has its challenges though. A team of caring, passionate, strong-willed self-starters can, at times, demonstrate a broader range of emotions than your typical workforce. People who care are deeply vested in outcomes and tend to wear their emotions on their sleeve, especially when things don't go according to plan. Such spirited teams will inevitably encounter moments of disagreement and discontent. Conflict must be brought into the open with direct, honest conversations that diffuse tension before it becomes toxic. Divergent views and spirited debates are always welcome, but mutual respect is required. Disagreements and debates sharpen our thinking, provided they're rooted in a genuine spirit of camaraderie and commitment.

During my time with the fire department, I earned a distinguished service award. The mayor presented me with a plaque that read, "No one cares how much you know until they know how much you care." Those words stuck with me. To this day, I still want the people around me to know how much I care.

After our business survived its first year—a feat I still consider miraculous—we had ten people on our team, all twenty-somethings. For some, it was their first job. We wanted to take care of our people, so Rachel and I negotiated with a benefits company to offer healthcare at a discounted group rate. After working out the details of our plan, we felt like a real company, and we were excited to present it to the team.

One Monday morning, a representative from the benefits company came in and walked the team through the healthcare package. For the size of our company, it was robust. There was a solid medical plan as well as dental and vision care. With such a young team, the benefits were priced aggressively, and we felt it demonstrated how much we cared.

Like every company that Rachel and I had ever worked for, the premiums would be paid primarily by the employees and deducted from their paychecks on a before-tax basis. We would subsidize some of the premium and bear the cost of administering the plan. Everyone on the team received an impressive blue folder with all the plan information and an enrollment form to be completed.

By the end of the week, not a single person had returned their enrollment form.

When we asked around, we got the same answer from everyone: "Thanks, but no thanks"—they wouldn't be enrolling.

Rachel and I were baffled. We couldn't imagine going without medical coverage when we started our careers.

We cared about our team. People working without medical coverage—that just didn't sit right. I thought through what we would do if someone on the team had a serious health issue, and I knew Rachel would be on the same page.

"What would we do if someone was diagnosed with a serious illness? Suppose they needed expensive treatment and had to be out for an extended period. Would we stop paying them?" I asked.

"Of course not!" Rachel said. "We'd keep paying them and help with the medical bills."

That night, we decided to pay 100% of everyone's insurance premiums to ensure that they were adequately covered—not just in the event they had a problem, but so they could also be proactive with their healthcare at little or no cost to themselves.

The next day, I told the benefits manager.

"You're crazy!" he cried. "I don't have a single client that pays 100% of their employee premiums. Look, Evan, offer to pay 20%. See if that's enough to get them onto the plan."

"We're trying to build something special here," I reminded him. "If we're going to create a family, we need to treat them like family."

Over a decade later, we still pay one hundred percent of the medical benefit premiums for all our employees and their families, and every year, we have the same argument with our benefits provider. Since the early days, we have added several new benefits, including a guaranteed match 401(k), online learning platform memberships, mediation and health app memberships, group discounts from other businesses, new technology—and much more. We're proud of the way we handle our benefits. It's part of our culture, and it shows the team that we have their backs.

Part of our culture is how we communicate. In an unstructured workplace, communication is critically important. If the Ops Team doesn't understand the Sales Team's priorities, neither team can execute with precision. When Product Development is out-of-sync with the Creative Team, packaging and product manuals get messed up, a potentially dangerous situation. If Finance isn't in tune with all the different initiatives across the company, we might fail to budget appropriately and find ourselves vulnerable.

Most companies keep different departments in separate silos, but we knew a strong communication flow across our company was essential to sustaining the culture we were all building. Communication encourages transparency and allows us to shift priorities quickly if necessary. Teams can drive projects forward, confident that their work won't be undermined by other projects headed in a different direction.

To encourage fluid communication and keep all departments on the same page, we've had an "all-hands" Monday lunch since the beginning of the company. It used to happen in my office with about six employees. Now, our weekly town hall fills our large office on an entire floor, with presentations simulcast to screens in overflow areas. For the first half-hour, everyone enjoys the catered lunch and uses the time to catch up or get to know people from other departments. In the remaining hour, each group reviews their priorities and shares useful intel with the group. Sales may offer highlights from retailer selling and meetings. Finance may share our recent performance. Operations may warn of upcoming challenges in the supply chain so that we can all plan accordingly. Before the end of lunch, everyone in the company is on the same page.

A motivated team, brimming with enthusiasm and empathy, guided with clarity and purpose, will create a workplace where remarkable accomplishments naturally unfold. Dash is now a living brand, with a workplace that has become a hub of growth, creativity, well-being, and community.

Takeaways
NO CULTURE, NO COMPANY

- **You get what you tolerate.**
  In any organization, the behaviors and attitudes that leaders and employees accept, consciously or unconsciously, set the tone for the entire workplace environment. Tolerating negativity, complacency, or unproductive behavior erodes morale and hinders progress. But when leaders hold themselves and others to high standards of professionalism, respect, and collaboration, they establish a culture where excellence is the norm.

- **Build a culture of excellence, not envy.**
  I love it when team members challenge me. I know I'm working with the right people when I sense they are way better at their jobs than I would be. I've created a team with diverse experiences and perspectives by surrounding myself with people whose strengths match my weaknesses. That diversity helps us quickly adapt to changing trends and market conditions, allowing me to focus on new opportunities and keeping us ahead of the competition.

- **Silos belong on dairy farms.**
  Not in companies determined to compete successfully in a dynamic and evolving marketplace. Our success demands a culture of open minds and open lines to encourage the quick, essential flow of know-how, intelligence, and information throughout the organization.

22. Trust and Empowerment Unleash Potential

To perform my best, I need two things: empowerment and trust. This goes back to my days as a firefighter and held true for every job I've had since. I need to be empowered to do my job and confident I have the trust of those around me.

When people don't feel empowered, they wait for instructions instead of doing what they know needs to be done. Micro-management prevails over progress. Change appears frightening, and inefficiency becomes the norm. Everyone's frustrated. The culture turns toxic. Inevitably, the smart people up and leave.

Without trust, great work is nearly impossible. Fear of making mistakes limits imagination as people pour more energy into making excuses than performing to their potential. A lack of imagination stifles creativity and innovation. The absence of trust creates a culture based on self-preservation rather than self-actualization, learning, and growth.

Why pay intelligent people and then fail to empower them? Why spend so much time choosing the right people if you aren't going to trust their judgment, initiative, and drive?

The typical American work week is five days of boredom salted with anxiety. Rachel and I wanted to create an environment that would be the antithesis of that.

We challenge our people to pursue remarkable outcomes in our quest for excellence. We empower them with the authority to do what they know is necessary and trust them to execute with boldness and purpose. As we offer guidance and assess their progress, the outcomes consistently surpass what's attainable in an environment of micromanagement.

Here on Planet Earth, things always go wrong, yet few companies are at their best when things don't go according to plan. But the right time to empower your people to be at their absolute best is when something goes wrong for a customer. All emergency responders know this; it's in their DNA. Retailers? Retail suppliers? Not so much.

There's no faster way to fail at winning hearts than neglecting a customer who needs help. And most retailers bungle this end of the deal, which results in waning customer loyalty, which the same retailers lament.

As a firefighter, I learned to expect everything to go wrong—emergencies never follow a script. Running a business, I naturally expect the unexpected. Empowering my team to solve problems as they happen means taking care of people when they need us most, which means outperforming our competition. Coming through for people has turned frustrated consumers into some of our most loyal brand advocates.

Almost every company understands the importance of addressing the problems faced by their consumers. However, most leaders fail to trust and empower their people to solve problems, which crushes their ability to deliver remarkable outcomes.

Shortly after founding the company, I bought a computer. I ordered it directly from the manufacturer and was excited to get it after waiting three weeks for a custom configuration. But when I plugged it in, it wouldn't turn on. I tried a different outlet and then a different power cord. No luck. The thing was DOA.

I called the customer service number and was put on hold for almost 20 minutes. When a human finally took the call, they listened to my problem. Then they started to "help."

"I'm going to need to walk you through some troubleshooting steps to determine if the machine is faulty," the customer service person said. "But first, I need to get the serial number."

"Can I give you my order number instead?"

"I'm sorry, sir. I will need you to provide the serial number of the machine. You can go into the settings, then info, and it will show you the serial number."

"Ma'am, I just explained that the machine won't power on."

I was starting to get frustrated.

"Okay, sir, you can turn the machine over and find the serial number on the label on the bottom."

My vision was pretty good, but it was impossible to read the tiny print on the label, so I used my iPhone to take a photo and then zoomed in to recite the number back to the agent.

"Okay, sir, I have that information now. I will need to walk through some troubleshooting steps with you."

"But I can't turn it on. It's dead!"

"Sir, I can't initiate a replacement until I confirm we went through this process," she said scoldingly.

"Go ahead," I sighed.

"Press and hold down the power button and then release it," she instructed.

I did as I was told.

"Nothing," I told her.

We went through all the steps I had already tried, things anybody who has ever used an electronic device would have tried. Finally, the agent admitted, "It seems you received a defective machine."

I was expecting her to commiserate just a little. To say that this never happens, or that it's highly unusual, and that she's sorry for the inconvenience. But her matter-of-fact tone made me think this happens frequently, which brought their brand's quality into question. And I was 15 minutes into the call and still hadn't heard an apology. She hadn't even apologized for my nearly 20 minutes on hold, which I had complained about when our conversation began.

"How do we initiate the replacement?" I asked.

"Uh, sir, I need to transfer you to the Returns Department."

By this point, I was close to delaminating. And it didn't get any better from there, as I waited to process the return before being transferred to the sales department to work on a replacement.

Few things fry me more than companies that don't care that they've wasted my time. We've all been there, right? Mine was by no means an extraordinary experience. And, in a way, I was grateful because it brought the need for empowerment into focus. I won't tolerate letting our customers down when they need us the most. Everyone on the team knows we are only in business because of our customers and must treat them accordingly. As a leader, it's my responsibility to set the right tone and build the guardrails, but to get the best results, I must empower and trust my team.

Our products' warranty typically runs for one to two years, but if something doesn't work, it doesn't work, and it is on us to make it right, regardless of where or when they bought it. In the product business, problems are going to arise. Rather than viewing the issue as a loss like most companies, we see the opposite. When a customer calls with a problem, it's an opportunity to win their loyalty.

Every time our support team gets involved, it's expensive. That's a fact. Most financial people would look at our level of expenditure for customer service and snarl. They see it as an expense to be trimmed. We see it as one of the most important investments we can make in our company's future. Many of our strongest advocates and brand evangelists are people who first came to us with a problem.

We don't provide excellent customer support because of unique training or processes. We provide exceptional service because our people care, and we empower them to do what *they* feel is necessary to make the customer happy.

When we started out, we used a shared customer service center. After six months of shipping products, we flew to California to meet with the customer service agents handling our account. We were eager to hear what our customers were saying and learn what we could do to offer them a better experience.

The agents were also working for several other large brands you know well. I started by asking them which brand they preferred to receive calls about.

The whole room immediately responded, "Dash."

I was skeptical, so I pressed for more information.

"You're the only brand that allows us to actually take care of the customer and use our discretion to make a situation right," one agent said. "That's why the customers we deal with love your brand."

Another agent told us, "When we answer the phone, the customer generally comes in hot. Okay, we expect that. They've been conditioned by years of frustrating calls with other brands. Most people assume they're about to get the run-around, so they immediately yell and carry on to get a resolution. But you allow us to defuse that anger right away before the call goes off the rails, so the rest of the conversation is calming, relaxed—even fun. And at the end of the call, the customer hangs up with an unexpected feeling that they were *heard*, their issue was taken to heart, and your company actually cares about them."

There it was: tangible evidence that empowering our employees and trusting their instincts makes a significant impact, particularly when things go wrong. Humans have an innate desire to tackle challenges, and it's deeply fulfilling when we're free to do what we believe is necessary to achieve the best results. Besides producing great outcomes, our team's ability to handle issues without managerial approval is why our turnover rate is a fraction of the industry average. Happy teams produce happy customers, which produces happy teams, creating a self-perpetuating cycle. The mutual satisfaction among our customer service team and our customers has deterred us from implementing more cost-effective AI chatbots. The human element brings a personal touch that fosters loyalty, and our culture of trust and empowerment truly brings out the best in our people.

As the business grew, we moved from a shared call center to a dedicated team. Our agents still follow a simple process—do what's right to make the customer happy. They speak in our brand voice, instilling confidence that they will fix the problem. Their goal is nothing short of resolution on the first call. Each agent uses our products at home to become intimately familiar with their function, allowing them to speak from personal knowledge rather than a script. Their ability to effectively troubleshoot issues has reduced our returns by over fifty percent, further reinforcing our decision to invest in people.

In our business, handling consumers is the easy part. Treat them right; they will almost always forgive you and champion your business. It gets more challenging when something goes wrong with one of our retail customers. With the consumer, there may be a few dollars on the line. With a retailer, it could be the future of a multi-million-dollar business.

When I worked in retail, I always favored the (relatively few) suppliers who were there for me when things went sideways. From the launch of our start-up, I was determined that we would be among those few. Maybe because, as a firefighter, I was trained to move toward bad situations while everybody else was moving away. Or because, in my retail days, I'd been left holding the bag when things went wrong. Or maybe my parents just instilled the importance of accepting responsibility when things go wrong. Probably all of the above.

One of the cardinal sins in our business is for a retailer to advertise a product in a catalog and then have the supplier miss the delivery. Hence, the product is unavailable when the catalog hits homes. It happened to me several times in my retail career. It's not just frustrating—it's damaging to the store's brand. Thousands of customers enter the stores looking for the product only to be told it never arrived—sorry!

Everyone has heard much about the supply chain problems of the early 2020s, but those problems have always existed. Delays just happen—they always have and always will. What is rare, however, is a supplier who calls proactively to warn a retailer that there will be a problem. It's even less common for a supplier to fall on their sword, apologize, and promise to work with the retailer to do whatever it takes to make the situation right.

The more common scenario is for the retailer to discover that the goods are not where they're supposed to be when needed. Then, it's on the retailer to frantically track down the supplier. It gets exponentially more infuriating if the retailer can't reach the supplier who caused the problem. You wouldn't believe how common this is—because running from a problem is way easier than running toward it.

We run toward it. Face it head-on. We do everything possible to minimize the risk for our retailers. If we can't deliver as promised, they'll find out from us. We give the maximum notice possible and demonstrate we are more on top of the things that matter most to them than any of their other suppliers.

As we built our operations team, we hammered this point home by treating the goods we sold as produce. In the banana business, the goods must show up on time, or they spoil. We built processes into our supply chain that allow greater oversight than our competitors, who operate without fear of an expiration date. By identifying problems early, we usually solve them.

We have so much up-to-the-minute intel on our supply chain and inbound inventory that if there's even a whiff of a problem, we usually have enough time to pull an item before the retailer's catalog or circular goes to the printer. We have done this when we were on the cusp of a late delivery of advertised goods because it's never worth risking your customers' business to salvage an order. Sounding the alarm when a problem is looming inspires retailer confidence and encourages them to steer more business our way.

Trust and empowerment are cornerstones for enduring success in any business where competition is fierce, and challenges are constant. Trust acts like an unspoken contract that binds teams and assuages fears. Empowerment is the fresh air that stimulates innovation and allows individuals to step beyond the confines of their roles and realize their potential. These two elements create a culture of collaboration, innovation, and achievement. In the evolving business landscape, where agility and adaptability are essential, cultures rooted in trust and empowerment will not only survive but will dominate their marketplace.

Takeaways
TRUST AND EMPOWERMENT UNLEASH POTENTIAL

- **Do the right thing.**
  Businesses that do right by their customers create a positive brand image and a strong, loyal following that is crucial for long-term success. I aim to hire adept problem solvers who default to doing the right thing for our customers, which in turn is naturally the right thing for the company. I trust my people to use sound judgment and empower them to take appropriate actions to deliver remarkable results. The strategy has led to countless word-of-mouth referrals, repeat business, and a competitive edge in the market.

- **Inspect what you expect.**
  Providing trust and empowerment is terrific, but it must be balanced with accountability. I need to trust my team. That's why I hired them. As a leader, I must ensure my expectations are being met. I had to learn when to step back and let the team operate independently and when to step in to provide direction and feedback.

  Expecting and inspecting became my leadership mantra to ensure the trust and empowerment I provided were harnessed as I intended. Inspecting what you expect isn't just about oversight; it's about making sure the team has everything it needs to deliver on expectations and then some. This approach enhances the sense of responsibility within the team and contributes to a culture of continuous improvement.

At Dash, inspecting what we expect has fostered a productive, engaging, and accountable work environment. Trusting people and expecting them to give their best frees them to actually give their best. Inspecting the work ensures they stay on the right path toward fulfilling the company's objectives.

23. Go the Extra Mile

Rachel and I traveled all over the world every year to meet with our manufacturers and international customers. After a grueling trip around the globe in January 2020, we returned to the United States just in time to catch the first news reports on the coronavirus outbreak. Rachel and I felt fine, but we decided to quarantine to make sure we weren't spreading a disease that we couldn't even test for.

As media attention intensified, I started worrying about the possibility of a global pandemic. On the first weekend of February, Rachel and I drove to Sam's Club in New Jersey and stocked up on food and cleaning supplies. We bought club-size packs of toilet paper and paper towels and joked they would make nice furniture in our apartment. We loaded up on Clorox wipes and hand sanitizer. We even bought three boxes of medical exam gloves and joked about what we would do with them.

We started planning, personally and professionally, for the possibility of an outbreak in the United States. I spoke to several friends and coworkers. Most were downplaying the situation. I hoped they were right, but my experience in emergency services taught me it would be irresponsible not to prepare for the worst.

After my panic attack in Italy, I'd promised myself that I would always keep a firm grip on the financial health of our company. If we were facing a pandemic, I knew there were new scenarios I needed to consider and model out. I spent the second weekend in February deep-diving into our financials and putting our working budget through a stress test. What if revenue dropped 20 percent? 50 percent? What if the country's supply lines shut down for weeks or months, and we couldn't ship anything? I thought I might experience the terror of a doomsday planner, but the process was reassuring and cathartic.

In the Great Recession of 2008, management's failure to adequately stress-test their business models led to the bankruptcy of numerous retail chains and the shuttering of thousands of stores. Iconic retailers—from Circuit City and The Sharper Image to regional staples like Fortunoff and Levitz—were among the first casualties before it spread to other large chains like Linens 'n Things.

When I worked at Linens 'n Things in the early 2000s, the company was thriving. A few years later, they were among the many victims of the financial crisis. During my tenure, I would have bet it was mathematically impossible for the company to become insolvent in such a short period. I was wrong and would not make this mistake with my own business.

If our revenue took a big hit or stopped altogether, I knew cash management would be our lifeblood. So, we built a strategy to stockpile cash and stay liquid through the next several months of uncertainty.

Next, we pulled the entire operations team together to review our inventory position and contingency plans if the coronavirus disrupted our supply chain. Then, we turned our attention to anticipating the issues we could expect from our Far East suppliers.

It was still February. I hoped we were being overly cautious, but the stakes were high, and contingency planning had always been a regular business practice. Planning offered a security blanket at a time when the scenarios we were simulating seemed far-fetched, so I never expected we would need to put the plan into action.

In the fire department, contingency planning was second nature. We didn't just develop the plans—we rehearsed them rigorously and involved other departments from other jurisdictions to ensure we would all know exactly how to work with one another. Taking a page from my old playbook, I contacted all the third parties involved in our business. I shared our plan with our banking team and asked them what other information they would need to feel comfortable with our approach. I also asked what changes we could expect from them if things got worse. Just the fact we were communicating proactively would support their confidence in us when things started to look bleak for the country.

We contacted our warehouse in California to learn what contingency plans they had in place. We could have the best-laid plans at our headquarters in New York, but business would grind to a halt if our warehouse couldn't ensure continuity. The complexity of running a distribution center and relying on a labor force working in close quarters was the most daunting challenge ahead of us.

When choosing a warehouse ten years prior, we had narrowed our choices to three. Then we did the opposite of what most companies would have done—we selected the most expensive, Motivational Fulfillment and Logistics Services. We didn't decide based on price but rather on expertise and capabilities. Most importantly, we chose them because we admired their people. They were just like us, committed and caring professionals who solved problems instead of running away. Now, facing a possible pandemic, I was glad to have them on our side.

After we checked in with all our service providers and acquired a clear sense of their continuity plans, it was time to turn our full attention to managing whatever the new environment would throw our way.

Rachel and I involved our team members throughout the planning process to help us think through various scenarios and catch potential problems from different angles. The two of us were confident in our approach and capabilities. We were also aware it was on us to lead by example and set the tone for dealing with what turned out to be unimaginable.

As March arrived, a severe outbreak in the United States became inevitable. Cases had started multiplying in Westchester County, 30 miles from our New York City HQ. Westchester would become ground zero for the coronavirus in the United States.

I had selected the Financial District of New York City as the location of our headquarters, primarily for ease of access. Trains and subways from Long Island, Westchester, New Jersey, and the Boroughs of New York City converged within two blocks of our office. The promise of an easy commute had helped us attract top creative talent in the tri-state area—but suddenly, our reliance on mass transit was starting to look like a curse.

Fortunately, we had built the company on tools powered by modern technology. We had no legacy systems or on-site servers. We could maintain business continuity from anywhere in the world. With tactical planning out of the way, we pulled our entire team together for an impromptu standup meeting. Rachel and I, along with our President, Glenn De Stefano, led the discussion.

It was always comforting having Glenn at our side. His arrival at the company in 2016 marked a pivotal moment in our company's journey. It was six years after our inception, and we had established a strong market presence as we barreled toward $50 million in annual revenue. We had fewer than twenty employees, and they all suffered from the chaos created by the startup mindset that Rachel and I continued to employ. This startup survivalist mindset, while instrumental in our early days, had begun to manifest as frustration across our organization. As we continued to chase every emerging opportunity, we left a trail of shifting priorities and undefined roles in our wake. Rather than enjoying the pride of our success, chaos, and frustration permeated every aspect of our business.

Glenn and I had worked together at Macy's years ago, before he moved into wholesale, where he climbed the ladder, eventually becoming president of a division of Lenox, the storied dinnerware company renowned for gracing tables from the White House to the Met Gala. With a wealth of experience running a large wholesale organization, Glenn became the beacon of stability we desperately needed. Our new president wasn't just a routine hire; he was a strategic move toward operational sophistication and sustainable growth. He brought a sense of order and a knack for problem-solving that was crucial for transitioning from a fast-paced startup to a more structured, scalable enterprise.

Fast forward four years, as the pandemic loomed, Glenn had become more than just a leader; he was our true partner in running the business. His management of our day-to-day operations earned him the admiration and trust of our team, who found him genuine and accessible. He introduced systems and processes designed to tame the once-unruly workflow and guide us to become organized and efficient, allowing creativity and innovation to thrive in a more structured environment.

As the team gathered around us in a circle, we spoke confidently but showed our vulnerability, letting everyone know we were anxious about the pandemic and worried it would worsen. We reinforced that we considered everyone family and we would never put our family in harm's way. We told them we would go fully remote for a two-day test that might extend several weeks.

When things look uncertain and scary, openness and honesty are more crucial than ever. I told the team we expected our business to suffer serious interruptions but that we had already spent weeks preparing for several scenarios with varying levels of disruption. Then I paused and directed my gaze around the circle, meeting eyes with everyone, one by one.

It was such a strange, almost surreal moment in the story of our company—the story of our nation, for that matter. We were all struggling to take it in.

"Okay," I told them. "I need you to listen to this part very carefully. No matter what happens for the foreseeable future, there will be no layoffs or furloughs. Everyone in this room's livelihood is secure."

I paused again to make sure my words sunk in.

"If things keep going as they seem, we might see some tough times ahead. We will all know people who'll be personally impacted in different ways. It may shake your confidence and cause you to worry. These times will be challenging enough, so we want to remove any stress about your job security. Your jobs are secure. We are financially sound. We have stress-tested our financials and can make this commitment with our full confidence."

The gravity of our decision was not lost on anyone in the room. For many reasons, it was an intensely emotional moment, and some people were welling up with tears. For us as leaders, it was a defining moment. We had to set the ultimate example—our people come first. Companies always say this. It was on us to prove it.

"We're making a big commitment to you," I told them. "In exchange, all we ask is for you to keep giving us your best work. I know we are better prepared than anyone in our industry. We will put more distance between us and our competition. We'll ramp up our marketing to let consumers know we are here to support them. Our mission has always been winning hearts. We need to keep this in sharp focus every day with everything we do. Millions of people are going to be cooking at home more than ever. We are *the only* healthy food prep brand, and people will rely on us."

That wasn't cheerleading; it happened to be the truth.

"When Rachel and I founded this company, we focused on winning hearts rather than financial goals. We believed that enriching the lives of others would lead to sustainable success. We must stay true to our approach and support our consumers during these tough times. We will enable millions of people to cook healthy meals at home, keeping themselves and their families safe. More people are going to experience our brand than ever before, and all of us in this room we are the brand. We created it. We embody it. As more people experience it, we will win their hearts."

That day was one of the most defining of our careers for Glenn, Rachel, and me. We showed that we had our team's backs and knew they had ours. That gave everyone confidence. That made the difference. Two weeks later, we saw the difference it made when we each received a beautiful bound book. Each page was a 'thank you' note from a team member with a picture of them holding a Dash product. Nothing could have made us prouder or feel better about our actions.

In many situations, I agonize over the right words to say. But saying the words is easy—living them is the real challenge. I was confident that our carefully laid culture of respect, communication, and caring would enable us to adapt and operate deftly in a business environment whose basic rules seemed to have changed radically overnight.

In the first years after founding the company, my anxiety was about whether we would survive. Years later, most of my stress came from the fear of losing the caring culture that had fueled our success. But people performed superbly as we adjusted to life in the COVID-19 era. The team embraced remote working, and as we expected, customers turned to us with a greater appetite for home cooking appliances.

Within a few months, we had accepted our new normal. After an initial sales drop, the business stabilized, and the team adjusted to remote work. But it was 2020, and something else was looming to knock the country further off-kilter.

This time, it was the civil unrest of 2020. It seemed every company was posting a bold statement on social media. As a group, we were anxious to do the same and publicly declare that we stand against racism and discrimination. Our management team crafted a statement. Beautiful words that came from the heart—but somehow, they didn't feel sufficient. The statement lacked substance. We needed to act before our words carried weight and meaning. Talk is cheap. We needed to *do* something.

I read other companies' statements and combed through the comments. Customers and followers demanded to know the specific steps being taken to fight systemic racism. Their questions were largely unanswered, a silence that provoked rage and toxic frustration in the comment streams. We needed actions first, a statement later. We had to walk the walk before we talked the talk.

When our department leaders explained my decision to delay our statement, it was unpopular with many on the team. People were upset that we would remain silent while deciding what actions to take. Several managers told me that certain team members were upset and perceived our silence as complicit. I quickly pulled the entire team together to address the situation head-on.

I explained my rationale and showed examples of other brands issuing statements that lacked substance. Then, I circled back to have open discussions with the people who were still upset with our strategy. Over the next two weeks, we had over 40 small-group sessions to brainstorm meaningful actions. We were determined to make an impact and set an example for other companies. Social responsibility has always been important to us; we routinely give back in ways that touch lives. We supported several charities, including breast cancer and pediatric cancer research. It was now time to look beyond our current efforts and focus on the communities we serve.

During those two weeks of small-group sessions, we homed in on causes the team felt strongly about supporting and identified three main areas to focus our efforts.

First, we would immediately donate to five different charities that support equality through a commitment to ending systemic racism. The team researched organizations individually and then presented the best candidates to the company for consideration. After vetting them, the group voted for the top five, who received immediate monetary donations.

Second, we looked beyond the monetary support to uncover opportunities for involvement in worthwhile organizations. We researched several groups, focusing on those we could immediately impact.

Third, because we are a food prep products company, we found related causes to aid. We identified several charities focused on feeding people in need and made immediate product donations to help those people prepare healthy home-cooked meals.

Our actions were on target, but this felt like a defining moment—an opportunity to go the extra mile. The culture we had built is all about going beyond what's merely *good enough,* and I craved something we could be proud of.

Glenn, Rachel, and I decided that one day each month, the entire team would refocus its efforts on doing good outside the company. Each team member received an additional 12 days of paid time off to get involved in initiatives to make our world a better place, marking the birth of our *Dash of Good* initiative.

We envisioned a movement anchored in grassroots authenticity, so Rachel and I stepped back and asked for volunteers to lead the *Dash of Good Committee*. This group became the torchbearers of our commitment. Several people joined and outlined a blueprint for our involvement in organizations and charitable causes that resonated with our values. They coordinated an educational series where industry experts illuminated subjects from systemic racism to nuanced product design considerations for assisting those with disabilities. Then, they facilitated volunteer opportunities, including tending to senior citizens, facilitating meals for those in need, and mentoring future leaders from underserved communities.

To formalize our commitment, we designated one day each month as a "Dash Day," when every employee engages in activities vetted by the Dash of Good Committee. At least once quarterly, our entire workforce unites for a singular, impactful activity to support our commitment.

Our Dash of Good initiative transcends corporate social responsibility. It's become a source of pride for the entire company, and the camaraderie fostered by these shared experiences is evident. The initiative amounts to a seven-figure investment and demonstrates that we are willing to put our money where our mouth is. The broad scope of our investment, coupled with the peer-led committee, reflects our deep cultural commitment to enriching lives.

During the first year of the pandemic, our workforce tripled, and Dash of Good became a cornerstone of attracting talent aligned with our values. Our ongoing commitment has strengthened our organizational dynamics. It has enriched our interactions, built stronger bonds, and kindled a sense of collective purpose that transcends our bottom line.

Takeaways

GO THE EXTRA MILE

- **Have a Plan B (and a Plan C).**
  It's the firehouse ethos because you never know what you'll find at the end of the siren-screaming ride. Strategic foresight isn't just about predicting expected challenges; it's about building resilience against the unpredictable. Planning provides a sense of purpose and direction. It helps the team define goals, set measurable objectives, and move in sync toward a shared vision of the future.

  Once contingencies were set, I could focus on our most valuable asset: our people. In turbulent times, employees who feel valued, supported, and secure in their roles can be productive and engaged.

- **Put up or shut up.**
  When leaders issue a bold statement on an important matter but fail to match talk with action, credibility flies out the window. It shatters trust, disheartens talent, and undermines the same leaders. As a leader, I strive to be modest in what I say but imaginative and generous in what I do. I always look for ways to go the extra mile. Dash of Good solidified our commitment to doing good and reinforced our mission across all aspects of our business.

24. Turning Solid Values into High Market Value

In 1990, I dove into my turnout gear then raced out of the station on my first emergency call. As a firefighter and then an assistant captain, I learned to measure success by the strength of the teams we build and the lives we touch.

The bustle of the corporate retail world clouded that vision for a while. Season after season, I chased someone else's vision of success until, one day, I found myself fired from Macy's and all alone. It wasn't just a job I had lost; it felt like a piece of myself. But in the miserable weeks that followed, I found a silver lining. The stress and uncertainty I experienced led me back to those fundamental truths from my firefighting days. With a new sense of purpose, I began a journey that would lead me to a level of success I had never imagined.

When I founded StoreBound in 2010, 20 years after that first emergency call at the fire department, my goal was not to build and sell a company. I wanted to do great work on my own terms. I wanted to create something that would make a difference in people's lives inside and outside the organization.

I believed a business based on solid values would become a valuable company. So, from day one, our strategy was simple: Win the hearts of our employees and customers to create robust, sustainable success.

That simple philosophy worked. In less than ten years, we topped over $100 million in annual sales and were just getting started. Years of hard work and investments were finally paying off. Our sales performance was among the strongest for our retail customers. Our social media following was the largest in our industry. The team we had built was, and is, world-class.

But success doesn't come without a cost. Long days, late nights, and endless travel come with the territory, but the most nerve-racking is the relentless financial risk. By 2020, Rachel and I personally guaranteed a $40 million loan for the company, meaning that we pledged all our assets as collateral to our lender. If things went sideways, the bank would take everything we owned—apartment, cars, savings, the company, and anything else they could get their hands on. The only business decision left would be whose parents we were moving in with.

The burden of our risk was always with us—like an unwelcome third wheel in our relationship.

At the end of 2016, we decided it was time to sell some of our equity in the business. The investor would eliminate our personal guarantee, repay the loans that Rachel and I made to the company, and compensate us for all the years we had worked without pay or well below our market value.

Shaping such a deal wasn't in our wheelhouse, so we sought outside expertise. After interviewing several investment banking firms, we decided on Consensus Advisors, a boutique firm with partners we clicked with and admired. We planned to take our time, become familiar with deal terms, and understand the range of possibilities. Our bankers reached out to several private equity firms, family offices, and strategic investors, and over the next year, we took more meetings than I can recall.

Several groups we met with came back with Letters of Intent, LOIs, outlining their investment offers. With multiple LOIs, we spent several months whittling down our list of possible partners. The team at Consensus put our interests first, not pushing us to make a deal we weren't comfortable with, a style reminiscent of my mom's approach to selling real estate.

After narrowing the field to a final four, we took more meetings, asked more questions, and negotiated various points in their offers. In each case, something led us to conclude that the deal wasn't right or the parties involved wouldn't make for great partners. We continued to take meetings and evaluate LOIs for almost three years but never found the right partners.

By the middle of 2019, we were experiencing another period of rapid growth, and the company needed more of our attention. One Friday afternoon, Rachel and I were talking about pausing the investment process when, like a sign from a higher power, the phone rang. It was Billy Busko, the lead partner working on our deal.

"Would you be interested in meeting with Groupe SEB?" Billy asked.

Groupe SEB is an iconic, eight-billion-euro housewares company headquartered in France and publicly traded on the Paris Exchange. The company started in 1857 as a tinware workshop in Burgundy and, 100 years later, became the global leader in housewares products, with powerhouse global brands like All-Clad, Krups, T-Fal, Rowenta, WMF, and many others.

"Of course!" I replied, beyond excited at the possibility.

So, in November of 2019, Rachel and I, along with our President, Glenn, and SVP of Marketing, Cat, traveled to

Lyon, France, and the modern, sprawling corporate campus of our potential suitor.

After a tour of their impressive Innovation Center, we were shown to the executive boardroom, where we would present Dash to their top management.

The conference room was larger than our entire office back in New York City. It was beautifully appointed and felt more like the setting of the United Nations General Assembly than a corporate boardroom. The sleek table went on and on and on, and I thought I might need binoculars to get a decent view of the people sitting at the far end. Each seat had a microphone and flat-screen display, which rose almost magically from the table.

Maybe I should have been intimidated by the setting, but it felt more like a homecoming. While working my way up the corporate ladder, I had several career-defining moments in rooms like this one. I was a different person now than the young, arrogant executive who got himself fired from Macy's. There had been bumps along the way and moments of panic, but we had created a living, breathing company that was dynamic and successful and reflected our deepest values.

Most people facing a defining moment in a conference room like this would focus their presentation on what they need. But I was thinking back on Tony Graziosi throwing me out of his office for making our meeting all about me. I would never make that mistake again, so I focused on *their* needs. I wanted them to see, as clearly as possible, what we Americans could offer to make them more successful.

As I sat at the head of the table in that magnificent room, my goal was to forge a partnership with the Goliath of our industry. I knew the impact our modern approach could have on their business. Dash would help them appeal to younger generations while providing insights into a new digital approach that every company was trying to figure out.

They were very astute people, so it didn't take long for everyone in the room to recognize the synergies. Our strengths were the opposite of theirs, which made us a great match. I acknowledged that their vast experience and resources were an obvious benefit for us and re-emphasized that our digital expertise and modern approach provided a window to an even more prosperous future for them. From the response around the table, it seemed everyone agreed that combining our strengths would be a win for both sides.

After the presentation, we gathered in their private dining room for a delicious lunch, complete with a cheese course, dessert, and *bien sûr*, a wine pairing. We enjoyed the delicious meal and took in the view of the French Alps, their snow-capped peaks visible from the dining room.

Over lunch, we spoke like old friends, with the possibilities before us creating mutual excitement. After lunch, their CEO indicated they wanted to structure a deal to acquire a slight majority ownership in our company. We would continue to operate as a standalone entity led by our existing management team, pursuing our same mission. It was the deal Rachel and I had been searching for.

We sat across from one another on the high-speed train back to Paris, our legs entangled, gazing out at vineyards as the TGV zipped through wine country. We occasionally made eye contact, smiling each time.

Finally, Rachel leaned toward me and whispered, "When we started, did you ever imagine—"

"Absolutely," I said. "I did. I always did."

And I meant it. While so many things seemed to go wrong along the way, we kept our focus on what we were building. Every win strengthened our resolve, and every setback strengthened it even more. We aimed to win hearts, and we won millions of them.

Several months later, in the press release announcing they had acquired 55% of Dash, Thierry de La Tour d'Artaise,

Chairman and CEO of Groupe SEB, said, "Groupe SEB is present in the daily lives of consumers throughout the world. Our objective is to always stay one step ahead and to accompany them as lifestyle and consumer habits change. This is why we decided to partner with Dash, which is inspiring millions of consumers to take steps toward healthier living. Dash's leadership in digital marketing has enabled their brands to gain strong favor with younger consumers and we are looking forward to supporting their innovation efforts. SEB is committed to helping Dash extend its leadership presence in the wellness economy and supporting Dash's mission of enriching lives."

For many entrepreneurs, taking on a partner means letting go of the enjoyment and excitement of running your own show. Our experience has been the opposite. Rachel, Glenn, and I continue to run our company. We lead a fantastic team. Business is exciting, evolving, and growing. We have highly supportive partners and access to resources we'd only dreamed of. And we remain laser-focused on our mission of winning hearts and making the world a better place. I still wake up each day, excited to get to work and shape our future.

In Loving Memory of Matthew Dash

You drew people to you like a magnet. Your giant circle of friends was a testament to the warmth, kindness, and genuine love you radiated. Your infectious laughter and boundless compassion left an indelible mark on everyone fortunate to have known you.

Your time on this Earth may have been tragically brief, but your impact on the lives of those around you was monumental. Your courage to follow your heart's true calling—helping others navigate the storms of life—continues to inspire me.

This book would not have come to fruition without you helping to shape the way I approach each day. I'm grateful to have called you my best friend and little brother for 44 years. Your legacy lives on; in my amazing niece, Gaia, in the hearts of your family, and in all the lives you touched along the way.

With My Deepest Gratitude

To all the remarkable individuals who have been, are, and will be part of the Dash family, your dedication, creativity, and passion inspire me every day. You are the heart of our collective success, and I am profoundly grateful for the opportunity to work alongside each of you in our constant pursuit of winning hearts.

And to all the retail buyers who believed in our mission and gave us a chance. There is no more humbling experience than seeing Dash products in your amazing stores around the world.

There are countless others who have been a part of our journey at Dash that deserve recognition for making us better businesspeople and human beings:

Thierry de La Tour d'Artaise, Stanislas de Gramont, Cathy Pianon, Bruno Labrosse, Oguzhan "Oz" Olmez, and all our friends at Groupe SEB: We are grateful for your belief in what we are building and for your endless support. We continue to learn from your passion, discipline, and expertise every day.

Yvonne Leung: You and your incredible team (Maggie, Eva, Mandy, Frankie, Andy, Queenie, Flora, and so many more) have been our eyes and ears 24/7 around the world. Your diligence and care allowed me to manage a few hours of sleep each night!

Tony Altman and Cheryl Nateran: For over a decade, your capable team has delivered our products with care and precision, allowing us to focus on our strengths and grow the business.

Laurie McCarthy and Ralph Natale: You and the team demystified how to move our goods around the globe. The credit you extended in our early days meant so much to us, and the holiday cookies are the best in the world!

Andy Tannenbaum, Charlie Sharf, Bob Gribic, and Ethan Rosenblum: You took a chance on us before we turned a profit and saved us from a predatory lender. Your capital was the fuel we needed to power our growth.

Billy Busko, Marshall Schleifman, and Betsy White: Thank you for your approach and patience in getting us the deal of our dreams. And Naz Zilkha, for helping us think through all the things we didn't want to think through on the way to closing our deal.

Greg Zucker: You are always there at the drop of a hat to help us navigate every legal issue. Your business-minded, practical approach to every situation gave us the confidence that we could deal with any situation.

Brian Belles: Your endless hours of IP counsel have been invaluable, and you somehow make every conversation enjoyable. I'm thankful to have you in our corner.

Lisa London: You helped us amass a wealth of trademark assets to protect our identity.

Phil Brandl and Derek Miller: You and the entire team at the IHA offered the most incredible platform for new brands to get a shot at connecting with the industry at a world-class show.

Ranco Pan, Lance Huang, and Jonathan Hsu: We manufactured our way into pop culture together!

Oscar Cantu and Vincent Sege: You helped us navigate foreign concepts and prepare for anything that might come our way. Your friendship, guidance, financial expertise, and stewardship are beyond appreciated.

Geoffrey & Margaret Zakarian and Anthony Candella: What a ride! Your standards and your passion have made us better at everything.

CJ Stafford: Thank you for caring for our customers as if they were your customers.

Dawn Langeland and Jack Barbour: Your creativity, diligence, and connections continue to keep us in the media around the clock.

Bill Buczak: You have been connecting people and showing me how to be a better version of myself for almost 3 decades. You're an example of how people make the difference, no matter the situation!

Bill Csaszar, Thomas Barndt, and all my former firefighting brothers: You accepted me as a cocky college kid and taught me lessons that helped me mature, and put me onto a path toward success.

Bev West: Your consultation on this book helped to pull out the real meaning of my stories and add color everywhere.

Peter Behrens: I didn't know if this book would ever come to fruition, and I can't thank you enough for helping edit my manuscript and for teaching me to hone my writing skills.

Daniel and Charlie Dash: You have been my biggest champions, and you rode so much of this ride with me as I wrote this story in real-time. Seeing you become the amazing men that you are is my greatest source of pride. And Daniel, the editing and guidance you provided on this book made it so much more than it was going to be. I love you guys more than you'll ever know.

Tahlia and Kacy Hecht: For being adorable models on our packaging, store displays, and marketing materials. It's easy to win hearts when people see your beautiful faces.

And finally, Cynthia and Geoffrey Hecht, not only are you the best in-laws, but you are terrific in-store merchandisers, always taking the time to make sure our products look great on the endcaps.